# Contents

# Chapter 1

## INTRODUCTION

Finance is a vital resource for every organisation and it is important that all staff, particularly managers, have an understanding of finance. Often this area remains the domain of a few, and non-financial managers may be excluded from detailed financial issues. This book is therefore written to help managers gain a basic understanding of key financial concepts that affect an organisation's day to day operations.

The public sector has undergone many changes in recent years with respect to commercialisation and accountability. These changes have included outsourcing, competitive tendering, Public Private Partnerships, and a general increase in public services being delivered by the private sector, to name a few. It is becoming increasingly important for all public sector organisations to demonstrate that they are financially viable entities in their own right. This means that income, regardless of its source, can fully support all expenditure, and that value for money services can be provided to meet the requirements of end users.

Ideally, managers should have some knowledge of finance such that the financial implications of service decisions are correctly taken into account. This book covers the most important aspects of financial accounting, enabling managers to have a greater understanding of the financial information presented to them and to assist communications with colleagues and finance professionals.

The text covers key concepts such as keeping the accounts, understanding financial statements such as income and expenditure, and the balance sheet. It also explains how cash flows are calculated and examines key financial performance indicators.

In addition to providing a practical text with illustrations, the book also incorporates exercises at the end of each chapter to enable readers to practice the techniques covered, and apply the concepts to their work situation. Suggested solutions are provided at the end of the book and the final chapter contains a glossary of key financial terms.

This book is one of a series of "Essential Skills for the Public Sector" titles. The series aims to assist public sector managers become more efficient and effective in carrying out their important management responsibilities. We consider this book to be an important part of the tool kit for public sector management development.

# Chapter 2

## KEEPING THE ACCOUNTS

## *Keeping Financial Records*

Organisations maintain financial records to keep account of all transactions, and it is these records which are used to develop the key financial statements. The two main statements produced by all public sector organisations are the "income and expenditure account" (similar to a profit and loss account for a private sector organisation), and the "balance sheet".

The income and expenditure account is a statement showing the surplus or deficit arising as a result of the organisation's activities over a period of time, for example a year. The balance sheet, on the other hand, provides a statement of assets and liabilities at a particular point in time, for example, the last day of the financial year. By deducting the liabilities from the assets, the balance sheet is able to establish the "net worth" of an organisation. Both these statements are discussed in more detail in chapters 3 and 4 respectively.

Maintaining proper financial records is essential for the following reasons:

❖ They provide the basis for the management accounts which are produced on a regular basis, monthly, quarterly, etc.

❖ They form the basis for the financial statements that have to be produced at least once per year

❖ They provide a record of what has actually occurred within the organisation in financial terms

❖ They are essential to ensuring accountability and protection against fraud

❖ They provide the information required for financial monitoring and control

❖ They provide an audit trail for each financial transaction that takes place

# *Financial Transactions*

Most organisations now operate some form of computerised financial recording system. Depending upon the organisation's size, this may vary from a large and powerful integrated real time system which handles far more than just financial data, for example, personnel information, to a system which is used solely for the accounting functions. A very small non-profit organisation, however, may be able to maintain their accounts on a computer spreadsheet. All financial recording systems, regardless of their complexity, are based on basic "double entry" book-keeping principles.

**Double entry** refers to the fact that each transaction requires two entries in the accounting system.

**Book-keeping** refers to the maintenance of accounting records which historically were kept in books or ledgers.

This book will not attempt to cover the theory of double entry book-keeping, however, it will illustrate the process for recording transactions using double entry principles with the following example.

*A school has set up a charity account to supplement its income for which separate records are being kept. Each transaction that has taken place is recorded in a red book, such that a set of charity accounts can be produced at the end of the year. The first month's transactions and the accounting entries that were made are given as follows:*

| Month 1 | Transactions | Accounting Implications | |
|---|---|---|---|
| 4th | Donations were received of £500 | Income increases by £500 | Cash increases by £500 |
| 9th | Models and toys were sold for £250 | Income increases by £250 | Cash increases by £250 |
| 10th | Prize for raffle was purchased for £100 | Expenditure on prizes £100 | Cash decreases by £100 |
| 14th | Raffle tickets were sold raising £500 | Income increases by £500 | Cash increases by £500 |
| 20th | An invoice of £50 was paid for the hire of stalls | Expenditure on hire charges £50 | Cash decreases by £50 |
| 27th | A new globe was purchased for the geography classroom for £100 | Expenditure on equipment £100 | Cash decreases by £100 |
| 28th | New equipment was purchased for the media classroom for £300 | Expenditure on equipment £300 | Cash decreases by £300 |

At the end of the month, it is possible to calculate the following:

- Total income for the month is £1,250 (£500 + £250 + £500)

- There has been expenditure on a range of items. Depending on the organisation, some of the expenditure would be regarded as capital expenditure whilst others would be classified as revenue expenditure (these terms are explained in Chapter 3)

- In this example, total expenditure is £550 (£100 + £50 + £100 + £300)

# *The Financial Statements*

As previously mentioned, the two key financial statements are the income and expenditure account and the balance sheet. These statements have to be produced at least once a year, and most organisations are required to have the statements audited by an independent auditor who provides an opinion as to whether or not the financial statements "present fairly", the financial position of the organisation for the period concerned.

The format of the financial statements will vary from organisation to organisation. However, there are standard terms and layouts, and the content of the statements should comply with accounting standards. An example format for the two statements is shown as follows:

## Income and Expenditure Account

|  | £'000 | £'000 |  |
|---|---|---|---|
| **INCOME** |  |  |  |
| Sales |  | 1,000 |  |
| Less: Cost of Sales |  | 400 |  |
| Gross Profit |  | 600 |  |
| Grants |  | 8,000 |  |
| Fees and Charges |  | 4,000 |  |
| Interest |  | 400 |  |
| Rent |  | - |  |
| Total Income |  | 13,000 | **A** |
|  |  |  |  |
| **EXPENDITURE** |  |  |  |
| Employee Costs | 5,500 |  |  |
| Transport Costs | 500 |  |  |
| Accommodation Costs | 2,000 |  |  |
| Goods and Services | 3,000 |  |  |
| Central & Support Service Costs | 400 |  |  |
| Sundry Expenses | 800 |  |  |
| Finance Charges | 200 |  |  |
| Depreciation | 300 |  |  |
| Bad Debts | 100 |  |  |
|  |  |  |  |
| Total Expenditure |  | 12,800 | **B** |
|  |  |  |  |
| Surplus for the Year |  | 200 | **A-B** |

## Balance Sheet Format

|  | £'000 | £'000 | £'000 |  |
|---|---|---|---|---|
| **Fixed Assets \*** |  |  |  |  |
| Land and Buildings |  |  | 4,250 |  |
| Plant and Machinery |  |  | 400 |  |
| Motor Vehicles |  |  | 1,300 |  |
| Equipment, Fixtures and Fittings |  |  | 800 |  |
| Total Fixed Assets |  |  | 6,750 |  |
| **Current Assets** |  |  |  |  |
| Stock |  | 0 |  |  |
| Debtors |  | 3,000 |  |  |
| Cash |  | 50 |  |  |
|  |  | 3,050 |  |  |
| **Current Liabilities** |  |  |  |  |
| Creditors |  | 2,000 |  |  |
| Overdraft |  | 800 |  |  |
|  |  | 2,800 |  |  |
| Net Current Assets |  |  | 250 |  |
| Less: Long Term Loans |  |  | (4,000) |  |
| **Total Net Assets** |  |  | 3,000 | A |
| **Represented by:** |  |  |  |  |
| Reserves b/f |  | 2,800 |  |  |
| Surplus for the year |  | 200 |  |  |
| Accumulated reserves c/f |  |  | 3,000 | B |
| (Net Worth) |  |  |  |  |

### A always equals B

\* Fixed Assets are stated after depreciation has been deducted from the cost

The above statements may sometimes be referred to by different names. For example, some public sector organisations call the "income and expenditure account" a "revenue account". Regardless of the name given to the statement, it will always show key features such as the surplus or deficit arising from the year's activities.

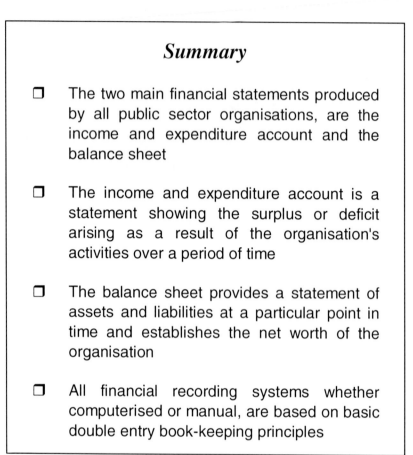

# Summary

❐ The two main financial statements produced by all public sector organisations, are the income and expenditure account and the balance sheet

❐ The income and expenditure account is a statement showing the surplus or deficit arising as a result of the organisation's activities over a period of time

❐ The balance sheet provides a statement of assets and liabilities at a particular point in time and establishes the net worth of the organisation

❐ All financial recording systems whether computerised or manual, are based on basic double entry book-keeping principles

# Exercise 1

## Accounting Entries

For the following scenarios identify the accounting entries, i.e. show which accounts will be affected.

For example, if a housing manager pays a builder £1,000 to undertake repairs, the accounting entries will be

*Increase in repairs expenditure account*  £1,000

*Decrease in asset of cash*  £1,000

a) A fire officer purchases new uniforms for £10,000 but has yet to pay the supplier.

b) A doctor charges £50 for writing a letter on behalf of a client for which the client had to pay in advance.

c) A school contracts out its cleaning services to a private contractor and has to pay £24,000 a year in monthly instalments. Show the entries for this month.

d) The planning department advised three clients during the week, all of whom were charged £200 each. Two paid immediately, however, the third has yet to pay.

e) Three managers of a day care centre service, decide to set up their own company in order to bid independently for contracts. To make the initial start, they all invest £10,000 each in the new company.

*For suggested solution see page 115*

# Exercise 2

## Financial Records

In order to gain an understanding of financial accounting within your organisation, undertake the following activities:

➲ Describe the type of financial accounting systems which exist in your organisation

➲ Is the system based on cash
accounting principles?     Yes ☐    No ☐
*(This means that throughout the year the
system only accounts for cash transactions;
that is it does not take account of debtors
and creditors, only those items which have
been paid for or income actually received)*

➲ Does the system operate accruals?
*(This means that income and expenditure*   Yes ☐    No ☐
*are accounted for as they arise and not as
they are paid for, i.e. debtors and creditors
are established throughout the year)*

➲ Does the system allow for
commitment accounting?     Yes ☐    No ☐
*(Does the system take account of orders
made but yet to be paid for)*

➲ Review a copy of your organisation's financial statements
ensuring that you understand all the headings used, and
their content. If there any questions about the financial
information that you would wish to ask, make sure you
contact the originator of the financial statements

# Exercise 3

## Which Financial Statement?

For each of the following items, identify which of the financial statements they belong to - the Income and Expenditure account (I&E), or the Balance Sheet (B/S); simply tick the appropriate boxes.

| | Income and Expenditure | Balance Sheet |
|---|---|---|
| Cash in bank | | |
| Fees | | |
| Motor vehicles | | |
| Creditors | | |
| Stationery | | |
| Rent | | |
| Grants | | |
| Overdraft | | |
| Computer maintenance | | |
| Depreciation | | |
| Debtors | | |
| Office furniture | | |
| Insurance | | |
| Loan | | |
| Bank interest | | |
| Salaries | | |
| Reserves | | |

*For suggested solution see page 117*

# Chapter 3

## THE INCOME AND EXPENDITURE ACCOUNT

The income and expenditure account reflects all the income "earned" by the organisation in a particular period, for example, one year. Income includes monies from all the activities and trades including any other income that may be earned such as interest earned on deposit accounts, investment income derived from investments, and rents earned from property. It also reflects all the expenditure incurred in pursuance of those trades and other activities.

The difference between the income and expenditure is either a surplus or a deficit defined as follows:

> **Surplus** ⇨ *Where income exceeds expenditure*
>
> **Deficit** ⇨ *Where expenditure exceeds income*

## *Elements of an Income and Expenditure Account*

The two simple definitions to remember in respect of income and expenditure are as follows.

*Income* ⇨ **what is earned by the organisation**

*Expenditure* ⇨ **what is used by the organisation**

The income earned in respect of the trades and activities and the expenditure used up in order to undertake the trades and activities, should be calculated over the same time period. This principle is called the "matching concept". Hence, all income for the year ending 31 March 20XX is matched against the expenditure for the same period in order to arrive at the surplus or deficit for the year.

Public sector and not for profit organisations can derive income from a wide range of sources. Many are publicly funded and therefore receive government grants or subsidies, others have to be self-sufficient and gain their income directly from the trade or activity which they are involved in. This means charging for services by contracting with other bodies or gaining revenues directly from the user.

Income tends to fall into the following main categories:

### Grants

Grants are often given by Central Government Departments, Non-Governmental Organisations, Charitable Trusts, Local Government and other grant giving bodies such as the Lottery Board. The level of grant received may vary each year depending on many external factors outside the organisation's control. Where the organisation is dependent on grant income they are subject to the terms and conditions of the grant giver.

## Fees and charges

Fees and charges may be levied for the use of services rendered. These could relate to one-off projects or may be the basis for a large proportion of the organisation's income, in which case a charging policy will be required. Fees may arise from providing professional advice, delivering training programmes, and so on, or charges may be levied for the use of services such as parking fines, and care services.

## Sales

This term tends to relate to the income derived from the sale of products as opposed to services. For example, ticket sales to events and sale of publications.

## Interest

Interest will arise from straight forward bank and building society deposits, money market deposits, etc.

## Rents

If the organisation has property which is used by a third party, it is normal to charge a rent for such use. In addition to rents, there may also be service charges if the property benefits from services such as heating and lighting of common parts, cleaning and so on.

## Dividends

Where an organisation holds investments, it will usually receive investment income. In the case of shares, this income is called a dividend.

The total income generated in respect of the organisation's principal activity is sometimes referred to as *"turnover"*, with the other income being referred to as *"other income"*.

When constructing an income and expenditure account, it should be noted that the income for a particular period relates to everything that has been generated in the period and does not necessarily equal the cash received. Quite often, monies due from a variety of sources such as customers and grant funders may be outstanding at any one moment in time; monies due and not yet received are referred to as **debtors**. This is illustrated by the following example.

*A doctors practice has a contract with the local health authority to deliver certain services for which a grant is given based on the number of registered patients. The practice also provides a range of other therapeutic services such as osteopathy and counselling for which patients have to pay. Income is also generated from the doctor's private patients. The grants due for the year are £240,000 paid in four instalments of £60,000 per quarter, the final quarter is always received in the month after the year end. All other fees and charges are paid on demand, but from time to time some credit arrangements are made whereby patients are given up to three months to pay their bills. During this year, the total bills raised by the practice totalled £640,000 of which £60,000 remained unpaid at the end of the year.*

*The actual income for the practice for the year is, therefore, £880,000, however, the cash received is only £760,000 as £60,000 of the grant and £60,000 of bills has not been received by the year end. This gives £120,000 of debtors.*

In the same way that income for a year relates to what is "earned/generated" as opposed to the "cash received" by the organisation, expenditure relates to what is "used" as opposed to the "cash paid". It is quite common for organisations not to pay their suppliers immediately even though the goods have been received or services used; monies due to suppliers etc. are referred to as **creditors**.

Day to day expenditure which is used up by the organisation as it delivers services is called **revenue expenditure**. This is distinct from **capital expenditure** which relates primarily to the purchase of fixed assets. The main categories of revenue expenditure can be summarised under these headings:

### Employee Costs
Including all expenses relating to employees, such as salaries, national insurance, pension contributions, car allowances etc.

### Transport Costs
Including all expenses relating to transport such as car leases, hire charges, travel, etc.

### Supplies and Services
Including expenditure on consumable items used in the delivery of the service, and other activities such as marketing, advertising and so on.

### Accommodation Costs
Including all costs relating to accommodation such as rent, rates, utilities, etc.

### Support Service Costs
Depending on the type of the organisation, there may be separate supporting services. These services typically include personnel, finance, legal, IT, and so on.

### Financing Costs
These costs relate to the cost of any borrowings made by the organisation such as interest and bank charges, and so on.

**Other Costs**
There are many general costs which may not fit into the
above categories such as subscriptions, sundries, etc.

There are generally two methods for recording transactions,
one is **cash accounting** and the other **accruals accounting**.
They differ in the following ways:

**Cash Accounting**
*Transactions are recorded when they have been paid or received, i.e.
when the cash transaction has taken place. This system does not
take account of debtors and creditors throughout the year. However,
at the end of the year a one-off adjustment is made with respect to
outstanding debtors and creditors at that point in time.*

**Accruals Accounting**
*Transactions are recorded as they occur as opposed to when they
have been paid for or received. This requires the identification of
accounts payable creditors) and accounts receivable debtors). By
operating accruals accounting, the full extent of income and
expenditure can be established throughout the year.*

# *Preparing the Income and Expenditure Account*

The income and expenditure account is a statement which may
be prepared at any time and for any period. It is usual that it is
produced at least annually, at the end of the financial year to
account for the activities that have taken place during the year.

To produce this statement, the organisation's books of account
will be "closed off" for the period or periods to which the
income and expenditure relates. To ensure that all the relevant

income and expenditure for the period is accurately reflected, adjustments may be made to some of the accounts. The types of accounting adjustments that are regularly made include the following:

### Accruals

An accrual has the effect of increasing the level of expenditure for items that have been used but have yet to be invoiced by the supplier. An example of this is telephone charges. If the telephone is used but not invoiced during the period of account, an estimate of the telephone usage cost for that period is accrued in the accounts.

### Debtors

Adjustments are made to income to reflect monies due for services rendered but not yet received. This has the impact of increasing income.

### Creditors

Adjustments are made for monies owing to third parties for goods and services received but not yet paid for. This has the effect of increasing expenditure.

### Prepayments

Like accruals, when monies have been paid in advance, then an adjustment needs to be made to reflect the advance portion. For example, at the end of March a telephone bill is paid which includes the line rental costs for March to June. This represents an advance payment or prepayment, and the telephone expenditure needs to be reduced by the amount of the prepayment.

### Depreciation

Where an organisation has fixed assets such as cars, furniture and fittings etc., the value of these assets need to be reduced to reflect the wear and tear encountered during normal usage. This is referred to as depreciation and is shown as an expenditure item.

**Bad Debts**

An organisation may have customers who fail to pay outstanding monies. The organisation may then be forced to create a provision for bad debts to reflect the possibility of non-payment or to write off specific bad debts from customers who fail to pay.

# Key Uses of the Income and Expenditure Account

All organisations are required to produce annual financial statements and therefore will produce an income and expenditure account at least once a year. The key uses of this statement are as follows:

❖ *It sets out the surplus or deficit made during the year*

❖ *It shows the key sources of income earned by the organisation*

❖ *It identifies the key areas of expenditure*

❖ *When compared with previous years it identifies areas of growth and reduction in both income sources and expenditure areas*

❖ *If targets are set in respect of income and expenditure levels, it can be used as a performance measure*

# The Trading Account

The trading account can be defined as an account of "one's trade". An account in financial terms refers to a record, and a trade refers to the principal activity. For many public sector organisations seeking to generate income and assess the viability of a service, then the use of a separate trading account may be useful. Where an organisation has many activities and sources of income and expenditure, the trading account differs from the organisation's main income and expenditure account in the following ways:

❖ *It only reflects the income derived from the trade*

❖ *It only reflects the expenditure incurred in relation to the trade*

Organisations that are multi-disciplinary may conduct several different trades or activities for which a separate account needs to be maintained. In some environments, the different trading or activity areas for which accounts are maintained may be referred to as a "business unit" account, or even a "cost centre".

Some organisations often have a main trade which is composed of a number of different trades with other activities being peripheral. This is shown in the following table.

| Organisation | Main Trade | Composite Trades | Other Activities |
|---|---|---|---|
| Local Authority | ■ Local public services | ■ Education<br>■ Social Services<br>■ Housing<br>■ Environment<br>■ Leisure, etc | ■ Renting commercial property |

| Organisation | Main Trade | Composite Trades | Other Activities |
|---|---|---|---|
| Department of Transport | ■ Land, sea, air transport | ■ Railways<br>■ Highways<br>■ Public Transport<br>■ Road and vehicle safety<br>■ Shipping<br>■ Aviation etc. | ■ Grant giving<br>■ Research |
| Revenues & Customs | ■ Collection of taxes | ■ Personal tax<br>■ Business tax<br>■ International tax<br>■ Valuations<br>■ Securities and investments, etc | ■ Public relations<br>■ Education |
| Hospital | ■ Patient care | ■ Out patient<br>■ Surgery<br>■ In patient care and accommodation<br>■ Research and laboratory<br>■ Pharmacy, etc | ■ Restaurant<br>■ Car park<br>■ Crèche |

Separate accounts may be established for each of the individual components of the main trade, and some of the other activities that an organisation may undertake. This allows the organisation to assess the financial performance of each component trade or activity.

# *Preparing the Trading Account*

As previously mentioned, the trading account is an income and expenditure account for a trade. In the public sector, the trade will most likely be a type of service, and often the income used to finance the expenditure on the service is derived mainly from public funds. This differs from a business whereby income is derived mainly from sales to third parties.

Expenditure relating to the trade has to be recorded and set against the income from the trade. In order to calculate an accurate trading position it is important to match like with like. Therefore, if expenditure on a particular area relates to several activities, it should be apportioned fairly between them and allocated to the correct trading account. This may be the case for expenditure items such as accommodation costs, where accommodation is being shared between several different trading activities.

An example trading account for a personnel department in a public sector organisation is shown as follows:

|  | £ | £ |
|---|---|---|
| **INCOME** | | |
| Charges to Clients based on time sheets: | | |
| ▪ Recharges to other departments | | 77,500 |
| ▪ Private Sector | | 45,000 |
| ▪ Voluntary Sector | | 40,000 |
| ▪ Advice to committee | | 5,000 |
| | | 167,500 |
| **EXPENDITURE** | | |
| Salaries | 104,800 | |
| Other Expenses | 14,500 | |
| Supplies and Services | 8,700 | |
| Controllable Expenditure | 128,000 | |
| Service Level Agreement Costs | 39,500 | |
| *(Share of costs charged by other departments allocated per number of staff)* | | 167,500 |
| **Net Surplus/Deficit** | | **NIL** |

The key to preparing a trading account is operating an effective accounting system, where expenditure and income items can be coded to the trade, and shared costs can be apportioned and allocated using fair criteria.

## *Objective of the Trading Account*

The main objective is to measure the performance of the trade or service. In this case, performance is usually measured in financial terms in the form of the trading result, i.e. whether a surplus or deficit is achieved. Depending on the organisation's objectives, each trade may strive to break even, where neither surplus nor deficit is desirable. Otherwise, there may be a desire to maximise surpluses or minimise deficits.

The performance achieved on the trading account can assist the organisation to answer the following questions:

### Is the trade viable?

*It is very important to establish if the trade can at least break even whereby the expenditure needed to deliver the service can be covered by the income generated by the service. If this is not the case, the organisation will have to consider to what extent it is prepared to support the trade from other funds.*

### Is the trade profitable?

*If the trade generates surpluses, it can assist in compensating for deficits and overspending experienced by other parts of the organisation. Also, surpluses may be invested in service development.*

## Is the service an income generator?

*The trading account will identify how much income can be generated by the trade. Generally, the income will tend to be externally supplied which may include grants, fees, charges, etc.*

## Is the trade suitable for competition?

*The trading account will identify the nature of income and expenditure required by the service, and hence if it would be the type of service that might be attractive to third parties wishing to compete to deliver the service. Also, the trading account will assist the organisation to identify what changes need to be made in order to make the service potentially suitable for competition. In the current climate of outsourcing and competitive tendering for many public sector services, this question is being asked far more frequently.*

# *Summary*

☐ The difference between income and expenditure is either a surplus or a deficit

☐ Public sector organisations can derive income from a wide range of sources. These include grants, fees and charges, sales, interest, rents and dividends

☐ The income for a particular period relates to everything that has been earned in the period, and does not necessarily equal the cash received

☐ Expenditure relates to what is used as opposed to the cash spent by the organisation

☐ The main types of expenditure incurred by most organisations include employee costs, transport costs, supplies and services, accommodation costs, support service costs, and financing costs

☐ At the end of the accounting period, in order to obtain an accurate reflection of income and expenditure, adjustments may be made to take account of accruals, debtors, creditors, prepayments, depreciation and bad debts

☐ The key to preparing a trading account is operating an effective financial accounting system

# Exercise 4

## Preparing a Trading Account

A new business unit has been established this year to provide communication services for which a separate trading account is required.

The cost of purchase and development of the appropriate equipment was £100,000 and a £100,000 loan was taken out to finance the purchase. The business unit provides a range of services which are sold to the public and private sectors.

Income for the first year included two contracts of £50,000 each from local authority departments and four contracts from other business units averaging £20,000 each. The direct costs related to contract sales represents 25% of the contract price. At the end of the year all expenditure items had been paid for, but 40% of the total contract fees due were outstanding.

The cost of running the unit is summarised as follows:

| | |
|---|---|
| Consultant fees | £20,000 |
| Salaries | £32,000 |
| Salary of a part time administrative officer | £6,000 |
| Office overheads | £6,000 |
| Other charges | £5,000 |

Interest on the loan is 5% per annum payable by the end of the year, and depreciation has been set at 15% on equipment

From the information provided, calculate the end of year trading account for the business unit, using the following pro forma.

|  | £ | £ |
|---|---|---|
| Income: | | |
| Fees | | |
| Expenditure: | | |
| Direct costs | | |
| Consultant fees | | |
| Salaries | | |
| Office Overheads | | |
| Other charges | | |
| Loan interest | | |
| Depreciation | | |
| Total | | |
| Surplus or Deficit for the year | | |

*For suggested solution see page 118*

# Exercise 5

## Preparing an
## Income and Expenditure Account

**Using the proforma on the following page, calculate the income and expenditure account for Limit H.A. a new social housing organisation.**

Limit H.A. has three trading accounts whose results are as follows:

|  | Housing Management Trading Account | Repairs and Maintenance Trading Account | Supported Housing Trading Account |
|---|---|---|---|
| Income | £1,200,000 | £300,000 | £450,000 |
| Less: Expenditure | £1,100,000 | £305,000 | £480,000 |
| Surplus/Deficit | £100,000 | -£5,000 | -£30,000 |

In addition, Limit H.A. earned £15,000 interest from bank deposits, and paid £65,000 in interest on loans owed by the organisation. There were central costs of £45,000 not allocated to specific trading accounts, and depreciation for the year was £10,000.

---

**Limit H.A.**
**Income and Expenditure Account**
**for the year ended 20XX**

**INCOME**                                                      **£**

Trading and Operations
Other income (interest)


**EXPENDITURE**

Direct Expenditure
Central Costs
Interest Payments
Depreciation


Surplus/Deficit

---

*For suggested solution see page 119*

# Exercise 6

## Preparing Your Own Trading Account

If applicable, prepare a draft trading account for your own section within your organisation. (This could be a division, business unit, cost centre, department, etc.)

**Calculate your income**   ☐ A
For example, external fees and
charges; internal recharges; budget
allocation; etc.

**Identify all areas of expenditure**
For example, salaries, rent, etc.

_____    _____
_____    _____
_____    _____
_____    _____
_____    _____
_____    _____
_____    _____
_____    _____

**TOTAL**   ☐ B

**+ Surplus/- Deficit for the year**   ☐ A-B

Remember income includes everything earned during the year, regardless of whether or not the cash has been received, and expenditure includes everything used during the year regardless of whether or not it has been paid for.

# Chapter 4

## THE BALANCE SHEET

### *The Balance Sheet*

The concepts of the income and expenditure account and trading account may be relatively straightforward, however, the balance sheet often remains a mystery. In order to fully understand financial accounts, it is important to understand both financial statements. A pro-forma balance sheet was set out in chapter 2. The key point to remember is that the balance sheet is a statement of *assets* and *liabilities* and the two sides must always balance. In other words:

$$\boxed{\text{Assets}} \quad = \quad \boxed{\text{Liabilities}}$$

remembering that assets are **owned** by the organisation and liabilities are **owed** by the organisation to someone else.

### *Types of Asset*

There are three main asset categories:

*Fixed Assets*
*Intangible Assets*
*Current Assets*

Other terms are sometimes used to describe assets, but these are generally alternative names for the three asset categories previously mentioned. Each type of asset is discussed in the following paragraphs.

### Fixed Assets

These assets include items such as land and buildings, equipment, fixtures and fittings, vehicles and plant and machinery.

All these items have an on-going value to the organisation in so far as they will last within the organisation for more than one year. How long these items do in fact last, varies considerably from one organisation to another and each organisation will adopt **depreciation** policies with respect to how long they expect the fixed asset to be of use. For example, if it is assumed that vehicles will have a useful life of 4 years, then it is normal for them to be depreciated over that time. One approach to depreciation is to adopt a straight line method and depreciate the asset equally by 25% each year. Alternatively, the depreciation charge may be calculated based on the reducing balance of the asset value each year.

For example, if a car was purchased for £12,000 and assumed to last the organisation 4 years, adopting the straight line approach, each year £3,000 would be written off the value of the car as depreciation. This would be shown as a depreciation charge in the income and expenditure account, and each year be reflected in the balance sheet as a reduction in the vehicle's value.

| Year | Vehicle Cost | Depreciation charge for the year | Accumulated Depreciation |
|------|------|------|------|
| Year 1 | 12,000 | 3,000 | 3,000 |
| Year 2 | 12,000 | 3,000 | 6,000 |
| Year 3 | 12,000 | 3,000 | 9,000 |
| Year 4 | 12,000 | 3,000 | 12,000 |

Different items in the organisation's fixed asset attract varying levels of depreciation. The deprecia will be the subject of the organisation's **depreciation**

It is normal practice to state all assets in the acc original cost at the time of acquisition. The actua asset will change over time, and it is often cc depreciation reflects the diminishing value that mo after they have been used. The calculation of der from an exact science and is often only an estimat in value. It is only if and when an asset is sold, th its true value can be established.

In some cases land and buildings appreciate in v depreciate over time, although this depends on t land and buildings in question (e.g. leasehold or f unusual to find that these items are not depr shown in the balance sheet at cost. If it is cor value of an asset has increased over time it is u a professional valuation to reflect its currer Revaluations can increase or decrease the ass the balance sheet.

Fixed assets are sometimes referred to as capi they are a result of capital expenditure. Wh

purchases an asset that has an on-going value, it is usually "capitalised", i.e. forms part of the fixed assets in the balance sheet. Any major additions to the asset can also be capitalised.

## Intangible Assets

Intangible assets are those which have no physical existence. They include items such as **goodwill**, the premium or excess value over and above the tangible worth of the organisation which a buyer is prepared to pay. It also includes items such as brand names, patents and trademarks. The valuation of intangible assets is often very subjective and therefore the accounting approach to these assets is to treat them prudently and to exclude them from the balance sheet as far as possible. Typically, this means writing off the value of intangibles, if not immediately, over a number of years.

## Current Assets

Unlike fixed assets, which generally are expected to stay within the organisation for at least a year, **current assets** by their nature are very changeable and tend to vary regularly within a year. The main types of current assets are:

• *Stocks; e.g. stationery, food stocks, materials; all of which change on a regular basis. Included in this category is "work in progress". Unlike a tangible stock item, this may have to be a subjective figure representing partly completed work.*

*Debtors; amounts owing from customers. Receipts can be obtained almost daily, hence, debtors go down, also invoicing can be carried out daily, hence, the value of debtors go up.*

*Investments; these represent short term investments, i.e. of less than one year duration. They may arise from surplus cash balances or may be part of a treasury*

*management strategy. They include interest bearing bank deposits, treasury bonds and so on. Some organisations may have long term investments which are usually presented as a separate asset category. Short term investments would often form part of an organisation's "liquid" assets, as they can be realised for cash very quickly. This is not necessarily the case for long term investments.*

❖ *Bank and cash balances; cash receipts and payments can be made daily, hence, cash balances fluctuate up and down accordingly. Bank and cash balances are the most "liquid" form of asset an organisation may have. Liquidity is discussed in the next chapter.*

# Liabilities

Liabilities represent everything that the organisation owes and are generally split between long and short term liabilities.

❖ *Long term liabilities are those that generally speaking will be outstanding for more than a year. For example:*

~ *Loans*

~ *Mortgages*

~ *Hire purchase agreements*

~ *Leases, etc.*

❖ *Short term liabilities are those which are generally repayable within a year. They primarily comprise of creditors and bank overdrafts. Creditors refer to the whole range of payments payable within the year such as:*

~ *Rents,*

> *~ Salaries,*
> *~ Interest charges,*
> *~ Suppliers,*
> *~ Loan repayments,*
> *~ Professional fees, etc.*
> *Bank overdrafts are a short term liability as they are repayable on demand*

Another important liability is any kind of investment made by the owners of an organisation, normally in the form of share capital. Share capital is a liability because it represents an investment into the organisation by the "owners", and is therefore **owed** by the organisation to the owners.

In many private organisations, **share capital** often represents a large injection of funds necessary to provide investment or working capital. When used in the public sector, however, share capital is often a nominal amount to reflect ownership. For example, it is quite common for the executive or management committee members to hold a nominal £1 share to reflect their "ownership" or legal "connection" to the organisation.

# *Reserves*

In whatever form they are represented, the total reserves represent the "net worth of the organisation". Each year's surpluses are added to the previous years accumulated reserves to arrive at the accumulated reserves for the current year. Similarly, any deficits are deducted from reserves and will reduce the level of accumulated reserves. Reserves are presented on the liability side of the balance sheet as shown below:

```
Assets
    Fixed                             X
    Current                           X
    Total Assets                      X   A

Liabilities
    Owners/Shareholders Funds         X
    Long Term                         X
    Short Term                        X
    Reserves                          X
    Total Liabilities                 X   B

                                    A = B
```

There are many terms used to represent different types of reserve, and examples are listed as follows:

**General Fund**
A term used for accumulated surpluses, or funds that can be used for any general purpose

**Capital Funds**
Reserves earmarked for specific future capital expenditure

**Restricted Funds**
These are reserves which have been specifically earmarked for a particular activity and hence are restricted for only that use; they may be separately identified such as the "asset replacement fund", or "staff development fund".

**Revaluation Reserve**
This is a common term representing the added value arising from the revaluation of an asset, usually land and property

**Owners' Equity**
Amounts invested by individuals in a private business

**Share Capital**
Amounts invested by stakeholders in an organisation which
is limited by shares. These companies can be profit making
or not-for-profit, but both types have limited liability.

Unlike loans, which are "owed" to the bank, reserves and
similar items are "owed" to the "owners" of the organisation.
In the case of a company, the owners would be the
shareholders, whereas for a public sector organisation the
owners could be the government or other relevant body
representing the public. For a voluntary or not for profit
organisation the "owners" would typically be the trustees or
those responsible for the organisation, who act in the role of
"trustee".

The surplus or deficit made each year is the main figure that
links together the income and expenditure account and the
balance sheet. The surplus shown on the income and
expenditure account reflects the results of the organisation's
performance for the year, which is "owed to" the owners of the
organisation, hence, it is represented as a liability on the
balance sheet.

# *Summary*

❐ The key principle of a balance sheet is that assets should always equal liabilities

❐ The three main categories into which all assets fall are "fixed", "intangible" and "current"

❐ Liabilities represent everything that the organisation owes. They include both long and short term liabilities as well as owners or shareholders' funds and reserves

# Exercise 7

## Understanding Assets and Liabilities

Make a list of all the assets and liabilities that your service area uses (even if it does not own them) and estimate their value.

| Assets | £ | Liabilities * | £ |
|---|---|---|---|
| | | | |
| Total A | | Total B | |

* Note: Reserves should be on this side although you may not be able to establish a realistic estimate for this item.

**Undertake the following net worth calculation:  A-B =** [ ]

# Exercise 8

## Preparing the Balance Sheet

Referring to the information in exercise 4, prepare the balance sheet for the Communications Business Unit using the proforma on the next page:

*For suggested solution see page 120*

# Communications Business Unit
# Balance Sheet

| | Cost £ | Depreciation £ | NBV £ | |
|---|---|---|---|---|
| **Fixed Assets** | | | | |
| Equipment | ☐ | ☐ | ☐ | A |
| **Current Assets** | | | | |
| Debtors | ☐ | | | |
| Cash | ☐ | | | |
| (**sub total x**) | | ☐ | | |
| **Current Liabilities** | | | | |
| Creditors | ☐ | | | |
| Overdraft | ☐ | | | |
| (**sub total y**) | | ☐ | | |
| **Net Current Assets (x-y)** | | | ☐ | B |
| Less: Loan | | | ☐ | C |
| **Net Assets** (A+B-C) | | | ☐ | D |
| **Represented by** | | | | |
| Surplus for the year from the trading account | | ☐ | | |
| **Net Worth** (D should equal E) | | | ☐ | E |

# Chapter 5

## KEY FINANCIAL PERFORMANCE INDICATORS

There are a number of financial indicators that can be beneficial in identifying an organisation's performance. Most indicators are compared with either a target for the current or previous year, to indicate increasing or decreasing performance. This chapter discusses some of the key indicators used by many organisations on a regular basis, and are of most relevance to public sector managers.

## *Surpluses*

Within the private sector reference is often made to "the bottom line"; this means the organisation's level of profits or profitability. For companies this is one of the most important measures of their performance. Within the public sector, the bottom line refers to the surplus or deficit made. This measure is also important within a public sector context, however, the degree of importance will vary with each organisation's objectives. For example, some public sector organisations have an objective to ensure that all their income is utilised during the year and therefore aim for a break-even position, whereby there are neither surpluses nor deficits. Others will have targets for surpluses to be made in order to build up reserves or funds for the future.

The surplus or deficit achieved by the organisation is identified on the income and expenditure account, produced at various stages during the year or at the year end. Individual activities within the organisation may also produce separate trading accounts which will show the surplus or deficit for that activity. Remember:

$$\boxed{\text{Income}} - \boxed{\text{Expenditure}} = \boxed{\text{Surplus or Deficit}}$$

One way in which surpluses can be used as an indicator, is to compare the **actual** surplus achieved with the **budgeted** surplus. Budgets will often be developed on a break even basis. A surplus will only result if the actual income exceeds the actual expenditure incurred. This occurs if more income is received than planned, or more usually, expenditure is below that budgeted. In some cases a surplus is not a positive performance indicator as it may reflect a reduction in the level of service delivered. Similarly, deficits may not necessarily be a negative indicator if they are supported by uncontrollable circumstances leading to increased output and levels of service delivery.

An example is given as follows:

| | | |
|---|---|---|
| Budgeted surplus for the year | £20,000 | |
| Actual surplus for the year | £15,000 | |
| Under-achievement | £5,000 | or 25% |

This shows performance as being 25% below target calculated as:

Actual Surplus - Budgeted Surplus    x    100%
Budgeted Surplus

A further use of surplus as a performance measure is to make a comparison with the previous year, for example:

| | This Year (£) | Previous Year (£) | Percentage Increase/ (Decrease) |
|---|---|---|---|
| Budgeted Surplus | 20,000 | 15,000 | 33% |
| Actual Surplus | 15,000 | 10,000 | 50% |
| Over/(Under Achievement) | (5,000) | (5,000) | 0 |
| Percentage | (25%) | (33%) | (8%) |

This table of figures shows that in both years, there has been an underachievement with respect to reaching the surplus performance targets. The monetary value of the under-performance has been £5,000 in both cases, but as the targets for each year were different, it represents a different rate of under-performance. The previous year was 33% below target whereas this year's performance was only 25% below target. The actual surplus achieved this year shows a 50% increase on the previous year, whereas the budgeted growth in surplus was only 33%.

*In summary, it is clear that although the performance target was not achieved in either year, this current year there was an overall 8% increase in performance compared with the previous year. (i.e. the underachievement reduced from 33% to 25%)*

This analysis can viewed in different ways, for example, it could be said that performance has been poor because this year's result was 25% below target, or it could be said that this year's performance has been good as there has been a 50% growth in surplus compared with last year and an 8% overall increase in relative performance.

# *Rate of Return*

The rate of return has always been an important measure in the private sector, and refers to the "return" on "investment" (ROI), or the "return" on "capital employed" (ROCE). The definitions of "investment" and "capital employed" can and do vary from organisation to organisation, however, usual definitions include the following:

### Net Assets
This figure is clearly stated on the organisation's balance sheet and takes into account fixed assets and net current assets.

### Owners Investment and Long Term Loans
This figure tends to be equivalent to the net asset figure

### Owners Investment Only
This figure will include any direct investment made by the owners of the organisation and any accumulated reserves and special funds. It does not take into account any debt being used by the organisation for its operations

### Capital Assets Only
This figure includes only the fixed assets

For the purpose of this text, capital employed is defined as being equivalent to net assets.

In the public sector, this measure has become increasingly important, when considering outsourcing options. That is, can the in house service provider deliver a better rate of return than an external provider? This will include the way in which assets are utilised in service delivery, as well as the contributions generated from the trading activities.

The rate of return achieved by any trading activity is important because it reflects the rate of income generated by a particular investment. If an activity's return on capital is less than that which could be achieved by investing the money in a bank or building society (i.e. a safe investment), then it may be considered unwise to take the risk and invest in the trade. Therefore, the target rate of return for the activity is usually set at a higher level than the ruling average rate of interest in order to reflect the risk. Most commercial companies establish their own internal rate of return reflecting their attitude to risk taking, particularly for new ventures.

The rate of return is calculated using the following formula:

$$\frac{\text{Profit or Surplus}}{\text{Capital Employed}} \quad \text{x} \quad 100\%$$

An example of this calculation is set out as follows:

A personnel division within a small police authority has been established as a business unit in preparation for tendering of the whole service. In

*51*

order to deliver the service, the following capital is required:

£

| | |
|---|---|
| Computer equipment | 100,000 |
| Office fixtures and fittings | 40,000 |
| Working capital* | 60,000 |
| TOTAL | £200,000 |

*\* This figure represents the capital needed to fund day to day operations due to the usual difference in timing between receiving the cash income and making payments for expenditure items. E.g. rent usually needs to be paid in advance. In the private sector this may be represented by an overdraft, in the public sector it is not usually so clear cut as each business unit does not have its own bank account.*

After a year of trading, the Personnel Business Unit achieved the following:

£

| | |
|---|---|
| Income | 400,000 |
| Less: | |
| Expenditure | 394,000 |
| Surplus | 6,000 |

The return on capital employed for the business unit is calculated by dividing the surplus achieved for the year by the capital employed by the unit, i.e. the original £200,000.

Rate of Return $\frac{6,000}{200,000}$ x 100% = 3%

Depending on the organisation's objectives, 3% may or may not be a satisfactory level of performance. For example, if a private sector organisation were to offer savings on the existing cost base, and at the same time freeing up the assets being used by the business unit (which could then be used elsewhere), then senior managers may consider it was essential for the personnel business unit to achieve a 6% rate of return to justify its continuing existence.

If a target rate of return has been established, and the capital employed is known (or estimated) at the beginning of the year, then the level of surplus required can be calculated. In this case the target surplus would have been £12,000, for a 6% rate of return.

Public sector organisations do not usually consider investing funds purely for a rate of return. Such organisations are funded to deliver services and hence funds should be fully utilised in this manner. However, how the resources are used to deliver services is a consideration. For example, it is possible to make a comparison of the service levels that can be produced from funds invested in-house, compared with the service levels achievable from a third party provider, from the same investment. In this case, the organisation can consider the rate of return in terms of service levels achieved, rather than in terms of the level of profit or surplus generated from the capital invested/employed.

# *Liquidity*

The level of liquidity is a performance measure reflecting the day to day efficiency in managing the organisation's cash flow. Liquidity levels are calculated by comparing the current assets with the current liabilities, i.e.

Current assets ⇨ including stock, debtors and cash

Current liabilities ⇨ including creditors and overdrafts

Within the public sector, the level of liquidity is often far removed from individual operational units, and is controlled centrally. Most public sector organisations, as with the private sector, will have timing differences with respect to cash receipts and cash payments, which have to be managed. If an organisation becomes illiquid, it means that it will have difficulty in making payments as and when they became due. This can often arise if a great deal of cash is tied up in the form of debtors, and hence cash balances are too low to pay all the outstanding creditors. In order to assist with cash flow, organisations may have to arrange overdraft facilities with their bankers.

There are two commonly used ratios to measure the liquidity of any organisation, these are defined as follows:

The "liquidity ratio":

$$\frac{\text{Current Assets}}{\text{Current Liabilities}}$$

This ratio should be in excess of 1.5 to demonstrate adequate liquidity.

The "quick ratio" or "acid test" is a similar ratio:

$$\frac{\text{Current Assets - Stock}}{\text{Current Liabilities}}$$

This ratio reflects only the cash and near cash current assets (i.e. debtors). Most public sector organisations have very little stock and therefore the quick ratio and liquidity ratio will be very similar.

This measure of performance particularly reflects the way in which an organisation manages its cash, a vital asset. A direct cost of mis-management could be the cost of having to use an overdraft - interest charged, or the lost interest on cash deposits. As the public sector increasingly faces demands for value for money, and often has to face funding constraints, liquidity will become more important when assessing performance.

For some organisations, there will be a need to ensure a more robust approach to raising income effectively and efficiently, with timely collection. This will require policies and procedures for debt collection, which are strictly implemented in order to maximise cash flows.

# *Other Financial Indicators*

There are other indicators which may be used to assess the financial performance of an organisation. The indicators identified below are most regularly used by the private sector, although still have relevance for the public sector.

## Debtor Days

Number of days taken for debt collection; from those who owe the organisation money. This is calculated in the following way. Firstly the "debtors turnover ratio" is calculated by dividing credit sales, (those where customers are given time to pay) by the value of the outstanding debtors at the year-end:

$$\frac{\text{Credit Sales}}{\text{Year End Debtors}} = \text{Debtors Turnover Ratio}$$

This ratio is then divided into 365 days:

$$\frac{365 \text{ days}}{\text{Debtors Turnover Ratio}}$$

Ideally, the resulting figure should be no more than 30 days. Longer collection periods may contribute to cash flow problems. This ratio is useful in relation to items such as rent collection. Firstly, the value of rents is divided by the year end rent arrears to calculate the rent turnover ratio, and then this ratio is divided into 365 days to calculate the average number of days for rent collection.

## Gearing

This relates to the level of long term debt used by the organisation. It is calculated using the following formula:

$$\frac{\text{Debt Level}}{\text{Net Assets}} \quad \text{x} \quad 100\%$$

Depending on the type of activity undertaken by the organisation, high levels of debt may indicate poor performance. In addition, high levels of debts will require a high level of revenue to support the resulting interest payments.

For the public sector, the financial indicators of performance will tend to concentrate more on the following:

❖ *Rate of increase or decrease in expenditure*

❖ *Levels of income generated from different sources, such as the amounts of grants claimed*

❖ *Amount of variance between actual and budgeted income and expenditure*

❖ *Level, rate and timing of income collection, such as rent arrears for housing organisations*

❖ *Unit costs of service provision*

❖ *Degree of achievement in respect of efficiency savings*

❖ *Value for money targets*

❖ *Amount of capital expenditure*

## *Summary*

❏ Within the public sector, the bottom line refers to the surplus or deficit made at the end of an accounting period. The desired level of surplus will vary from one organisation to another

❏ The rate of return has always been an important measure in the private sector and has become increasingly important to public sector organisations, especially those making important decisions, such as whether or not to outsource a service.

❏ The level of liquidity is a performance measure reflecting the day to day efficiency in managing the organisation's cash flow

❏ Other indicators used to assess financial performance, include debtor days; gearing; increases and decreases in income and expenditure; budget over and under-spends

# Exercise 9

## Calculating Key Financial Ratios

A legal services business unit have produced the following financial accounting information for the last two years.

| TRADING ACCOUNTS | | |
|---|---|---|
| | Year 1 £ | Year 2 £ |
| **INCOME** | | |
| Fees - internal recharges | 500,000 | 550,000 |
| Fees - external work | 100,000 | 150,000 |
| Total | 600,000 | 700,000 |
| **EXPENDITURE** | | |
| Salaries | 400,000 | 440,000 |
| Supplies and services | 80,000 | 100,000 |
| Overheads | 50,000 | 80,000 |
| Recharges | 54,000 | 63,000 |
| Total | 584,000 | 683,000 |
| Surplus for the year | **£16,000** | **£17,000** |

In addition, the unit used £100,000 worth of assets in the business both years.

## a) Calculate the following ratios which represent financial performance

|  | Year 1 | Year 2 |
|---|---|---|
| Return on Capital Employed | | |
| Surplus as a percentage of income | | |
| Income growth year on year | | |

## b) What other information would you wish to have in order to assess the business unit's performance over the two years.

....................................................................

....................................................................

....................................................................

....................................................................

....................................................................

....................................................................

....................................................................

....................................................................

....................................................................

*For suggested solution see page 122*

# Exercise 10

## Interpretation of Financial Ratios

Two local health centres have been asked to provide some financial statistics which set out their respective financial performance for last year. The figures given are as follows:

| Health Centres | 1 | 2 |
|---|---|---|
| • Surplus for the year | £5,000 | £600 |
| • Surplus as a percentage of total income | 1% | 0.2% |
| • Return on capital | 10% | 2.5% |
| • Liquidity ratio | 1 | 2 |
| • Debtors level as a percentage of total income | 30% | 20% |
| • Debtor days | 110 days | 73 days |
| • Percentage variance on surplus (actual compared with budget) | -50% | -10% |
| • Increase in productivity | 0.5% | 6% |

*From the above information, you have been asked to give your interpretation of the figures and advise which one of the health centres should close.*

*For suggested see page 123*

# Chapter 6

## THE IMPORTANCE OF CASH FLOW

## *How Cash is used in the Organisation*

Organisations have to undertake transactions in order to engage in any kind of trade. Goods have to be purchased, staff have to be paid, and therefore cash is essential in order to operate and survive. Cash receipts arise from a number of sources, for example, grants, fees, rents, etc. Cash payments are made for a variety of purposes relating to the organisation's activities. This incoming and outgoing of cash is generally referred to as **cash flow**. In addition to the conduct of transactions, cash has many uses in the organisation. These are:

### Investment
*Cash can be invested in terms of bank deposits or be used to purchase other items which can be invested. Investments usually yield a "return". For example, in the case of a bank deposit the return takes the form of interest, whilst in the case of an investment in shares the return would be a dividend.*

### Provisions
*It may be necessary to make a provision for known and sometimes unknown future events. For example, there may be a need to make staff redundancies. Cash balances can*

*therefore be set aside in order to meet future redundancy payments.*

Cash forms part of every transaction with the exception of certain accounting adjustments for which there are no cash implications. For example, depreciation, bad debt write offs, and so on.

# Timing of Cash Flows

The timing of incoming and outgoing cash is important in order to manage cash balances. There are a number of reasons for this, and they are summarised as follows:

## Limited or no overdraft facilities

*If an organisation has an overdraft facility, it is usually limited to a maximum amount and cash balances must be maintained within this overdraft limit. Some organisations have no overdraft facilities, as banks may not be prepared to lend in certain cases. This is especially true of many smaller not-for-profit and voluntary sector organisations, which some banks may view as high risk, even if they are delivering services on behalf of larger public sector bodies.*

## Minimising costs

*If cash balances are depleted and overdrafts are used, there will be a cost implication as most overdrafts carry a high rate of interest. Careful cash management can minimise the level and frequency of the overdraft and hence reduce costs.*

## Maximising income

*Surplus cash balances are usually invested, this is discussed in more detail under treasury management. However, careful cash management will result in more cash being available for investment and hence the potential for higher earnings.*

## Reputation

*Poor cash management can result in the organisation being unable to make payments when they are due. This leads to a poor image with suppliers if they have to wait over the due date for payment. It may even lead to suppliers ceasing to make supplies to the organisation, or withdrawing credit and hence requiring cash on delivery. Not having credit terms with suppliers can severely affect cash flows, as cash has to be paid out immediately, instead of after 30 or 60 days (the usual credit terms offered by suppliers).*

## Going concern

*If the organisation is to remain a **going concern** and not face the possibility of closure, it has to ensure there is sufficient cash available to make payments when they fall due. If cash flow becomes a severe problem, it may lead to suppliers taking legal action and ultimately forcing closure of the organisation. Further if salaries are not paid, employees could withdraw their labour, causing significant difficulties and potential closure.*

The timing of incoming and outgoing cash flows can be affected by a number of factors as shown in the following table:

| Source of Cash In | Factors affecting Timing |
|---|---|
| Grants | Much of the public sector is funded by grant. The timing of this receipt can be affected by the speed at which claims are submitted, or by the efficiency or otherwise of the grant giver in processing the claim. It is usual for an annual grant to be received in phases over the year, e.g. quarterly. Cash flows are particularly affected if grants are received in advance or in arrears. It can mean the difference of several months of having either positive or negative cash balances. |
| Fees/ Charges/ Sales | As with commercial organisations, the public sector sometimes transacts with the general public or other bodies whereby a sale is made or a fee charged. For example, local authorities raise some income by levying local taxes. These charges have to be collected. Cash flows are affected by the speed at which cash is received. It can be difficult to persuade customers to pay quickly, and it is quite common to offer payment arrangements and credit terms. The timing of receipts from third parties will depend on the efficiency with which the organisation implements its collections policies. These policies may include incentives for early payers, discounts, and legal action for non-payment. |
| Rents | It is usual to require a tenant to pay their rent in advance. In the case of commercial buildings rents are usually paid quarterly, whereas for residential letting rents are paid weekly or monthly. Even though a rent is levied in advance, in practice, the cash may not be received on the due date. Again, collections policies will affect how quickly cash is received. |
| Interest | Interest is earned on cash deposits if they are invested strategically. Current account balances often attracts low levels of interest. Effective treasury management can maximise this source of income, by ensuring cash is invested wisely for the correct periods of time according to cash flow requirements. Treasury management is discussed in the next section. |

| Source of Cash In | Factors affecting Timing |
|---|---|
| Loans | These usually relate to a specific activity such as the purchase of a property. It is not uncommon within the private sector for a company to take out a loan to assist with day to day working capital, especially in a development stage. The factors affecting timing include when the loan can be drawn down, e.g., whether all at once or in phases, and how the loan money is to be used within the organisation. |

| Source of Cash Out | Factors affecting Timing |
|---|---|
| Salaries | These payments have to be made regularly, usually at the end of a month or a week, depending on the terms and conditions by which staff are employed. Due to the nature of these payments, there is little that will affect the timing of this particular cash outgoing. In some organisations bonuses are paid, the timing of such payments being dictated by pre-set in-house rules and procedures. |
| Suppliers | There are many factors that affect the timing of these payments. It is usually to an organisation's advantage to delay paying suppliers for as long as possible to obtain a cash flow advantage. Most suppliers will offer credit terms, particularly to established organisations. These terms usually allow a number of days to pay, e.g. 14 or 30 days is quite common. Organisations sometimes exceed these terms, depending on their existing cash balances. A small supplier may find it has little bargaining power with a large customer, and in such cases the organisation may dictate the payment terms. As public sector organisations have a public image and reputation to preserve, most will try to adhere to the agreed supplier credit terms. In some instances, suppliers may offer discounts for prompt payment, and this may also affect the timing of payments. |
| Rents | The timing of these payments will be dictated by the lease agreement. It is normal for rents to be paid in advance. |

| Source of Cash Out | Factors affecting Timing |
|---|---|
| Interest | The timing of interest payments can be negotiated with the lender. The level of interest paid will relate to the type of lending being arranged. In some cases loans carry fixed interest payments over the period of the lending, however, interest on overdrafts often vary directly with bank base rates and therefore fluctuate. |
| Loans to third parties | Loans are made at the organisation's discretion and hence the timing at which payments leave the organisation can be closely controlled. It is usual for a repayment schedule to be given to the borrower, along with interest charges, such that incoming cash flows can also be predicted. |

In order to assist with cash flow management, it is normal to produce a cash flow forecast each year and to use this as a monitoring tool. The cash flow forecast is discussed in detail in the next chapter.

# *Treasury Management*

This is the term given to the cash management function in an organisation. The aim is to maximise the income that can be generated from cash deposits and to minimise the cost of any form of borrowings. Effective treasury management will depend on the investment and borrowing strategies used. For some public sector bodies these will be limited by legislation and recommended practice. For example, levels of borrowing may be restricted or the types of investment that can be made limited to those which carry the lowest risk.

## Investment strategies

Key investment strategies have been identified as follows:

❖ *Keep current account balances to a minimum and invest surplus cash in a deposit account, even if only for overnight.*

❖ *Depending on the amounts of cash available, longer term investments can be considered. The length of time for which cash can be invested will be dictated by the cash flow forecast, which will indicate when cash is required by the organisation. Generally, a higher rate of return can be obtained for longer term investments.*

❖ *Risk is related to reward so the investment strategy should be developed based on the level of risk the organisation is prepared to take. If it is a low risk strategy, then investments will be limited to "safe" investments such as bank deposits, treasury bonds with a fixed return, and so on. Investments in stocks and shares have a much higher degree of risk but scope for greater returns, and are generally not recommended as a prudent investment for public funds.*

❖ *Interest rates change daily and hence need to be monitored closely. Those responsible for treasury management should research a range of alternative sources in the market place, in order to achieve the best possible rates.*

❖ *The type of institution in which monies are invested is also important. Whilst no bank or institution is immune from possible failure, a publicly funded organisation should seek to invest funds with reputable organisations with a good track record, to minimise the risk of possible loss*

❖ *The timing of creditor payments is also part of treasury management, as the longer cash is retained within the organisation, the more scope there is to earn interest from it. However, in the public sector there are often time limits within which creditors must be paid. In some cases creditors offer discounted costs for early payment or some creditors may levy interest charges in the case of late payments.*

# Borrowing strategies

Borrowing can generally be split between short term and long term. Short term borrowing includes overdraft facilities, loans payable within one year, and other short term financing arrangements. This method of borrowing tends to attract higher interest rates. Long term borrowing usually attracts lower interest rates and is over a specific term. Treasury management activities concentrate on providing for the day to day cash needs of the organisation and planning to ensure that future cash requirements can be met. It includes investing surplus cash to maximise income, or arranging facilities to borrow funds which minimise costs.

❖ *The borrowing strategy may be affected by internal policies with respect to borrowing. These policies may limit the amounts that can be borrowed, and the lending organisations that can be used.*

❖ *The treasury manager will seek to minimise the cost of borrowing by researching the market place to obtain the best interest rates. Advice may also be sought from financial advisers and fund managers*

❖ *A cash flow forecast will identify the level of cash balances over a period of time and will help to*

> *highlight where negative cash balances may occur. This enables the organisation to arrange any necessary borrowing facilities well in advance.*

Cash balances should be monitored regularly as they may be subject to daily change. The person responsible for treasury management is required to make appropriate decisions as to how to invest surplus cash, or how cash short falls should be funded.

# Summary

❑ An organisation's incoming and outgoing cash is generally referred to as cash flow

❑ The timing of cash flows is important in order to manage cash balances. This is particularly necessary if an organisation's cash movements are large in terms of volume or value. The impact will affect the ability to minimise costs and maximise income

❑ Treasury management is the term given to the cash management function within an organisation. It serves the purpose of maximising the income that can be generated from cash balances, and to minimise the cost of borrowing

❑ To enhance cash flow, there are a number of investment and borrowing strategies which can be employed, which are usually determined by the organisation's level of acceptable risk.

# Exercise 11

## Understanding Your Cash Flow

### Complete the following questionnaire

**1)     Where does your cash come from?**

     a) Grants (50% - 75%)              ❑

     b) Grants (excess of 75%)         ❑

     c) Fees/earned income excess of 50%   ❑

     d) Total mixture, or varies each year   ❑

**2)     Does your organisation have an overdraft facility?**

     a) Yes               ❑

     b) No                ❑

**3)     Is there anyone in the organisation responsible for treasury management?**

     a) Yes               ❑

     b) No                ❑

**4)     Do creditors ever chase for payment?**

     a) Yes               ❑

     b) No                ❑

     c) Sometimes          ❑

**5)     Are salaries paid regularly and on time?**

     a) Yes               ❑

     b) Sometimes           ❑

     c) No                ❑

**6)**   **Are there ever freezes on expenditure during the year?**

    a) No ☐

    b) Sometimes ☐

    c) Yes ☐

**7)**   **Is there a high level of overdue debtors at any one point in time?**

    a) Yes ☐

    b) No ☐

**8)**   **Does the organisation have high finance costs?**

    a) Yes ☐

    b) No ☐

**9)**   **Does the organisation generate interest income from investments or positive cash balances?**

    a) Yes ☐

    b) No ☐

**10)**   **Calculate the liquidity ratio for the organisation (net assets/net liabilities). Is it...**

    a) Under 1? ☐

    b) Between 1 and 2? ☐

    c) Over 2? ☐

*For scoring results see page 124*

# Chapter 7

## FINANCIAL PLANNING AND CONTROL

Financial planning involves looking ahead at all the organisation's financial requirements, and identifying how they can be met over the time horizon being considered. The financial requirements should be based on the organisation's business plan objectives, hence linked directly to service delivery. The business plan is usually based on a higher level "corporate plan", which sets out the vision and medium to long term strategy.

The financial plan will set out the level of income required to meet the expenditure needs of the organisation for both revenue and capital items, and the different sources of that income. The plan will also consider the cash flow implications of the expected timing of income receipts and expenditure payments. This will assist in identifying the need for additional cash resources at particular times, if required.

A robust financial plan is essential to financial control. The plan provides a benchmark against which performance can be measured during the course of the year.

The financial planning process should include the following stages:

> ⇨ Setting the objectives for the organisation
>
> ⇨ Identifying and forecasting the expenditure levels needed to deliver those objectives
>
> ⇨ Identifying and forecasting the income sources available to fund the expenditure
>
> ⇨ Producing a forecast income and expenditure account
>
> ⇨ Identifying and forecasting the timing of cash flows, and resulting cash requirements

Each stage of the process is discussed in the following paragraphs.

# Setting Objectives

All organisations should undertake a process of setting realistic, time related objectives. Objectives will identify the type, quality and quantity of service to be provided. This is often undertaken as part of a business or service planning process. It is essential for public sector organisations to set targets with respect to service delivery for the future. These plans will usually cover at least one year, or perhaps a longer period.

# Forecasting Expenditure

Having set objectives, the organisation should then determine the level of expenditure required to meet them. Depending on the organisational structure, expenditure forecasts may be prepared by divisions, business units, service cost centres, etc. The forecast will consider how much needs to be spent for each area of expenditure over a specific timescale. An example of how these figures are constructed is shown as follows:

| Key Expenditure Headings | Process for developing forecast figures |
|---|---|
| Salaries | This will be based on the number of staff employed and current salaries, the terms and conditions of employment, the level of increments, pay awards, and bonuses. Other costs will also include the employer's national insurance and pension contributions. It should also reflect known potential joiners and leavers during the year. For example, if there is currently a vacant post, the forecast for the following year should reflect the timing of when that post will be filled. Salaries will be paid monthly, (wages perhaps weekly). The forecast should reflect the level of expected monthly payments, taking into account the changes to salaries levels that will occur throughout the year. |
| Other Employment Costs | In addition to salaries, there may be other employment costs such as car allowances; child care allowances; travel costs; and so on. Other payments sometimes made on behalf employees include subscriptions to professional organisations. All of these payments should be subject to accurate forecasting. |
| Transport | This forecast should be based upon the number and type of vehicles used and the average cost per journey. Previous year statistics will prove a useful starting point for this. These vehicles may include taxis, coaches, leased cars, etc. |

| Key Expenditure Headings | Process for developing forecast figures |
|---|---|
| Accommodation | Accommodation costs such as rent, rates, etc. are usually fixed for a number of years, and hence the expenditure on this area can be accurately forecast. Even if accommodation requirements change, such changes are usually planned and the new accommodation costs known well in advance. There are also other variable costs, such as service charges, cleaning contracts, maintenance contracts, and so on. Many of these can still be forecast accurately by agreeing future rates and charges with the service providers in advance. |
| Supplies and Services | This is probably one of the most difficult areas to forecast as it is difficult to predict what goods and services may be required during the year. However, to create an accurate forecast, the following should be used:<br><br>● the detailed action plan to be implemented during the year<br>● the planned expenditure for the year, for which estimates should be sought from suppliers<br>● the profile and nature of expenditure in the previous year, and list of unplanned expenditure, identifying which items where one-off, and which items are likely to recur<br>● the level of variance (difference between actual and forecast) experienced in the previous year, for each area of expenditure<br><br>The monthly forecast will reflect the peaks and troughs in expenditure, and guess work should be kept to a minimum, i.e. figures should be developed on sound assumptions. |

| Key Expenditure Headings | Process for developing forecast figures |
|---|---|
| Support Service Costs | In some organisations, support services, such as legal, finance, and personnel may be supplied by in-house departments. Alternatively they may be supplied by third party contractors. When developing the forecast, ideally an estimate of these costs for the year should be gained from the service provider, along with the method of payment. These estimates should be subject to negotiation such that the best rates are obtained. |
| Finance costs | These costs reflect the cost of borrowing, which may include a loan or the use of overdraft facilities. The cost of loans is usually fixed, or governed by clear terms and conditions over the term (period) of the loan. These costs can therefore be calculated accurately. The cost of using overdraft facilities is more difficult as overdraft levels fluctuate, and interest rates may vary depending on the amount of the overdraft at a particular point in time. Estimates can be made by preparing a cash flow forecast which identifies monthly overdraft requirements throughout the year. Other finance costs may include the costs levied for banking transactions. Banks tend to regularly inform customers of their charges and so estimates of these costs can also be made. |
| Other expenditure | There will be other expenditure items which do not fit strictly into any of the above categories. On the whole the best way to forecast these is to use prior year profiles of expenditure for similar items, or to obtain estimates from suppliers and providers for new items. It is usually prudent to include a miscellaneous or contingency sum in a forecast to take account of miscalculation and unforeseen expenditure items. |

For most public sector organisations, staffing will often be the largest area of expenditure.

# *Forecasting Income*

Developing an income forecast can be far more difficult than an expenditure forecast. The receipt of grants may be predicted, and once agreed a payment schedule is usually given. However, income from charges, fees, and so on can be very difficult to predict as these items will be largely determined by third party demand which is outside of the organisation's control. Therefore, income forecasts require assumptions to be as prudent as possible.

The following table gives examples of how income forecasts can be developed for public sector organisations:

| Key Income Headings | Process for developing forecast figures |
|---|---|
| Grants | The most difficult aspect of forecasting grants is predicting the level of grant that will be awarded in a particular year, as some grant givers do not determine their grant awards until very near the start of the financial year in question. To assist with the process, an estimate should be made of grant income based on previous year levels, inflation rates, and any known changes that might be made. Where specific grant income is exactly balanced against specific expenditure, there is a nil impact on the forecast. |

| Key Income Headings | Process for developing forecast figures |
|---|---|
| Fees and Charges | Many public sector organisations charge a fee for some of the services they provide, or levy a charge. Where these services are demand led, forecasting the level of income from this source is extremely difficult. It relies upon an accurate forecast of prospective demand over the forecast period, along with the mix of services that will be used. Such figures can be obtained by undertaking research into future trends, and analysing historic trends. If there is no available data, any estimates of such income should be very prudent, and reflect the lowest levels of expectation. Fees to be generated under contract are more straight forward as they should be agreed in advance with the service user/customer. For example, a local authority refuse collection service may have contracts to remove waste from commercial premises. |
| Sales | Sales tend to refer to products as opposed to services where the term fee is more common. Forecasting sales has the same difficulties as mentioned above for fees and charges, and the same approach should be adopted. |
| Rent | Some organisations have properties which can generate rents. This allows for accurate forecasting of rental income, as each unit will tend to have a fixed rent or rent increases will be set in advance. |
| Interest | Income arising from investments will vary depending on the level of investments made. Long term investments will often have a fixed rate of return or be linked to variable bank interest rates which can be estimated. The cash flow forecast will enable these levels to be estimated and hence help with the accuracy of the interest forecast. |

# *Income and Expenditure Forecast*

An example of a traditional format for an income and expenditure forecast is developed from the following assumptions:

A 20 place local authority nursing home is this year about to offer 25% of its places to fee paying private clients. It also has to establish a trading account so that its financial viability can be managed with a view to future competitive tendering. In order to assist with the process, the home has produced an income and expenditure account based on the following assumptions.

- An annual grant is received for £600,000. This will be paid quarterly in advance

- Fees of £1,000 per month are charged for each private place. It is assumed that only four out of the five places are filled for the year

- Fund-raising activities raise £12,000 for the year, from two main events, one in the Summer and one in the Winter

- Employee costs are £480,000, with no joiners or leavers during the year

- Operational costs are estimated at £12,000 per month

- Support service costs are estimated at £2,000 per month

The income and expenditure account is set out on the following page.

## Income and Expenditure Forecast

| | Apr | May | Jun | Jul | Aug | Sep | Oct | Nov | Dec | Jan | Feb | Mar | Total |
|---|---|---|---|---|---|---|---|---|---|---|---|---|---|
| **Income (£'000)** | | | | | | | | | | | | | |
| Grant | 150 | | | 150 | | | 150 | | | 150 | | | 600 |
| Fees | 4 | 4 | 4 | 4 | 4 | 4 | 4 | 4 | 4 | 4 | 4 | 4 | 48 |
| Fund-raising | | | | 6 | | | | | 6 | | | | 12 |
| Total | 154 | 4 | 4 | 160 | 4 | 4 | 154 | 4 | 10 | 154 | 4 | 4 | 660 |
| Expenditure (£,000) | | | | | | | | | | | | | |
| Employee costs | 40 | 40 | 40 | 40 | 40 | 40 | 40 | 40 | 40 | 40 | 40 | 40 | 480 |
| Operational costs | 12 | 12 | 12 | 12 | 12 | 12 | 12 | 12 | 12 | 12 | 12 | 12 | 144 |
| Support service costs | 2 | 2 | 2 | 2 | 2 | 2 | 2 | 2 | 2 | 2 | 2 | 2 | 24 |
| Total | 54 | 54 | 54 | 54 | 54 | 54 | 54 | 54 | 54 | 54 | 54 | 54 | 648 |
| Net Surplus/Deficit | 100 | -50 | -50 | 106 | -50 | -50 | 100 | -50 | -44 | 100 | -50 | -50 | 12 |

This type of forecast can easily be prepared using a spreadsheet program and should be accompanied by detailed assumptions showing how the figures have been calculated.

The forecast can then be monitored when undertaking financial control procedures. The total figures can be used as the annual budget, and the monthly forecasts can be used for management control purposes in the same way as a profiled budget (a budget which has been analysed on a monthly basis, taking account of seasonal and other timing issues).

# Cash Flow Forecast

The cash flow forecast is developed using the income and expenditure forecast. It reflects the timing of income receipts and expenditure payments and shows their impact on the organisation's cash balances. The purpose of the cash flow forecast is to assist in financial control and treasury management. It helps the organisation identify when cash shortages and surpluses are likely to arise such that the appropriate arrangements can be made.

The cash flow forecast looks similar in appearance to the income and expenditure forecast shown previously, however, the figures will not necessarily be the same. As with the income and expenditure forecast, the assumptions made in respect of estimated timing of receipts and payments need to be set out. Most importantly, any income not received before the end of the financial year is referred to as "debtors", and similarly outstanding expenditure payments are referred to as "creditors". Receipts from debtors and payments to creditors will be reflected in the following year's cash flow.

*For example, if income of £5,000 due at the end of the financial year is not received, it will then be shown as a debtor in the year end accounts. If it is likely that the cash will be received in the following year, it can be reflected in the following year's cash flow forecast.*

Given the income and expenditure example shown earlier, a cash flow forecast can be developed based on the following assumptions:

- The grant is paid quarterly in advance
- Fees from private clients are received monthly in arrears
- Money from fund-raising is all received in the month that it is earned
- Salaries are paid at the end of each month
- Operational costs are paid 2 months in arrears
- Support service costs are paid monthly at the beginning of each month

| | Apr | May | Jun | Jul | Aug | Sep | Oct | Nov | Dec | Jan | Feb | Mar | Total |
|---|---|---|---|---|---|---|---|---|---|---|---|---|---|
| **Income (£'000)** | | | | | | | | | | | | | |
| Grant | 150 | | | 150 | | | 150 | | | 150 | | | 600 |
| Fees | | 4 | 4 | 4 | 4 | 4 | 4 | 4 | 4 | 4 | 4 | 4 | 44 |
| Fund-raising | | | | 6 | | | | | 6 | | | | 12 |
| Total | 150 | 4 | 4 | 160 | 4 | 4 | 154 | 4 | 10 | 154 | 4 | 4 | 656 |
| **Expend. (£,000)** | | | | | | | | | | | | | |
| Employee costs | 40 | 40 | 40 | 40 | 40 | 40 | 40 | 40 | 40 | 40 | 40 | 40 | 480 |
| Operational Costs | | | 12 | 12 | 12 | 12 | 12 | 12 | 12 | 12 | 12 | 12 | 120 |
| Support Service Costs | 2 | 2 | 2 | 2 | 2 | 2 | 2 | 2 | 2 | 2 | 2 | 2 | 24 |
| Total | 42 | 42 | 54 | 54 | 54 | 54 | 54 | 54 | 54 | 54 | 54 | 54 | 624 |
| Balance month | 108 | -38 | -50 | 106 | -50 | -50 | 100 | -50 | -44 | 100 | -50 | -50 | 32 |
| Cash b/f | 0 | 108 | 70 | 20 | 126 | 76 | 26 | 126 | 76 | 32 | 132 | 82 | 0 |
| Cash c/f | 108 | 70 | 20 | 126 | 76 | 26 | 126 | 76 | 32 | 132 | 82 | 32 | 32 |

It can be seen from the cash flow forecast, there will be positive cash balances each month if the assumptions prove to be accurate.

There will also be a debtor of £4,000 in respect of fees not yet received and a creditor of £24,000 in respect of operational costs not yet paid. Some months have significant balances, peaking in January with a balance of £132,000.

# *Financial Control Techniques*

There are a number of control techniques that may be adopted to ensure the organisation is able to meet its financial targets. These include:

❖ *Monitoring income and expenditure forecasts*

❖ *Monitoring cash flow forecasts*

❖ *Calculating variances and taking action to correct adverse variances*

❖ *Undertaking re-forecasts to reflect the impact of actual figures on the future*

Some organisations may distinguish between revenue (income and expenditure**Error! Bookmark not defined.** on day to day operations), and capital forecasts (income and expenditure on long term assets), such that they can be monitored separately.

It is advisable that financial forecasts are reviewed monthly or quarterly. This includes updating forecast figures with the **actual** figures achieved for the period. New estimates are developed for the future months in order to reflect current events, changes in assumptions, and corrective action. As a result of these adjustments, a projection of the likely financial **outturn** at the end of the year can be made. This allows for the prediction of the likely year-end financial position, and assists with long term planning.

# Summary

☐ Financial planning involves looking ahead at all the financial requirements of the organisation, and identifying how they can be met over the time horizon being considered

☐ In order to control finances, there needs to be a plan to start with, otherwise there is no benchmark against which to measure performance over the year. Control, therefore, has to be within a framework which is set by the "financial plan"

☐ Public sector organisations should set targets with respect to future service delivery. This should identify the type, quality and quantity of service to be provided

☐ All forecasts require assumptions to be made, and income assumptions should be as prudent as possible because unlike expenditure which can be subject to a certain amount of internal control, income is often subject to external market forces

☐ There are a number of control techniques that may be adopted in order to ensure financial targets and objectives are met over time.

# Exercise 12

## Preparing an
## Income and Expenditure Forecast

A nursery school has 35 places which are subsidised by a grant of £48,000 per year. Fees are collected from parents on a weekly basis of £100 per week. The grant is expected quarterly in advance whereas fees are paid at the end of each week. Further income is derived from fundraising events such as raffles, fetes, sponsored walks, etc. These tend to net £200 per month. Donations are also obtained from local companies, and it is hoped that £1,200 will be raised during the year. Salaries tend to be static throughout the year at £13,000 per month. Catering costs are £1200 per month and uniforms of £2,000 are purchased in September and March each year. Toys and playthings average at £4,800 for the year and other supplies and services are approximately £1,000 per month. The rent of £20,000 is paid quarterly in advance and includes all accommodation costs. Other miscellaneous expenditure is £500 per month (this includes petty cash, staff expenses, etc.).

**Using the following proforma prepare the income and expenditure forecast based on the above information. (Assume 4 weeks in each month.)**

*For suggested solutions see page 126*

## Nursery School Income and Expenditure Forecast

| | Apr | May | Jun | Jul | Aug | Sep | Oct | Nov | Dec | Jan | Feb | Mar | Total |
|---|---|---|---|---|---|---|---|---|---|---|---|---|---|
| **INCOME** | | | | | | | | | | | | | |
| Grant | | | | | | | | | | | | | |
| Fees | | | | | | | | | | | | | |
| Fundraising | | | | | | | | | | | | | |
| Donation | | | | | | | | | | | | | |
| Total | | | | | | | | | | | | | |
| **EXPENDITURE** | | | | | | | | | | | | | |
| Salaries | | | | | | | | | | | | | |
| Catering | | | | | | | | | | | | | |
| Uniforms | | | | | | | | | | | | | |
| Toys | | | | | | | | | | | | | |
| Supplies & Services | | | | | | | | | | | | | |
| Rent | | | | | | | | | | | | | |
| Miscellaneous exps | | | | | | | | | | | | | |
| Total | | | | | | | | | | | | | |
| **Surplus/Deficit** | | | | | | | | | | | | | |

# Exercise 13

## Preparing a Cash Flow Forecast

With respect to the nursery schools financial position outlined in exercise 12, the following further information is given.

• Catering is paid in the month of supply, along with miscellaneous expenses

• All other suppliers are paid one month in arrears

• On average only 80% of parents fees are received on time with the other 20% being paid one month in arrears

• Half the donations appear to be received around Christmas and the other half in March

**Complete the pro-forma cash flow forecast for the nursery**

*For suggested solutions see page 127*

## Nursery School Cash Flow Forecast

|  | Apr | May | Jun | Jul | Aug | Sep | Oct | Nov | Dec | Jan | Feb | Mar | Total |
|---|---|---|---|---|---|---|---|---|---|---|---|---|---|
| **RECEIPTS** | | | | | | | | | | | | | |
| | | | | | | | | | | | | | |
| | | | | | | | | | | | | | |
| | | | | | | | | | | | | | |
| | | | | | | | | | | | | | |
| **PAYMENTS** | | | | | | | | | | | | | |
| | | | | | | | | | | | | | |
| | | | | | | | | | | | | | |
| | | | | | | | | | | | | | |
| | | | | | | | | | | | | | |
| **TOTAL** | | | | | | | | | | | | | |
| **Bal. Month** | | | | | | | | | | | | | |
| **Bal. b/f** | | | | | | | | | | | | | |
| **Bal. c/f** | | | | | | | | | | | | | |

# Exercise 14

## Re-forecasting

The nursery described in exercises 12 and 13 have had 3 months of operation and the actual cash flow figures are shown in the following proforma. The fundraising committee have not organised any events to date, but intend to get back to monthly activity as from August. The quarterly grant payments seem to be coming a month later than they should do. All other payments are following the original cash flow projection pattern, with the exception of supplies and services which have increased to an average of £1,200 per month, and catering which has decreased by £200 per month.

The nursery requires a re-forecast cash flow taking into account the above changes and they wish to know how much their overdraft facility needs to be.

**Use the proforma to undertake the re-forecast calculations.**

## Nursery School Cash Flow Re-forecast

|  | Apr | May | Jun | Jul | Aug | Sep | Oct | Nov | Dec | Jan | Feb | Mar | Total |
|---|---|---|---|---|---|---|---|---|---|---|---|---|---|
| **RECEIPTS** | | | | | | | | | | | | | |
| Grant | | 12,000 | | | | | | | | | | | |
| Fees | 11,200 | 14,000 | 14,000 | | | | | | | | | | |
| Fundraising | | | | | | | | | | | | | |
| Donation | | | | | | | | | | | | | |
| Total | 11,200 | 26,000 | 14,000 | | | | | | | | | | |
| **PAYMENTS** | | | | | | | | | | | | | |
| Salaries | 13,000 | 13,000 | 13,000 | | | | | | | | | | |
| Catering | 1,000 | 1,000 | 1,000 | | | | | | | | | | |
| Uniforms | | | | | | | | | | | | | |
| Toys | | 400 | 400 | | | | | | | | | | |
| Supplies & Services | 1,200 | 1,200 | 1,200 | | | | | | | | | | |
| Rent | 5,000 | | | | | | | | | | | | |
| Sundry | 500 | 500 | 500 | | | | | | | | | | |
| Total | 19,500 | 16,100 | 16,100 | | | | | | | | | | |
| | | | | | | | | | | | | | |
| **Bal. Month** | -8,300 | 9,900 | -2,100 | | | | | | | | | | |
| **Bal. b/f** | 0 | -8,300 | 1,600 | | | | | | | | | | |
| **Bal. c/f** | -8,300 | 1,600 | -500 | | | | | | | | | | |

**Overdraft facility should be £** [ ]

*For suggested solutions see page 128*

# Exercise 15

## Your Own Financial Forecasts

**If possible complete the pro-forma income and expenditure, and cash flow forecast with figures from your own organisation. If you do not have accurate figures estimates will do.**

## Income and Expenditure Forecast

| | Apr | May | Jun | Jul | Aug | Sep | Oct | Nov | Dec | Jan | Feb | Mar | Total |
|---|---|---|---|---|---|---|---|---|---|---|---|---|---|
| **INCOME** | | | | | | | | | | | | | |
| | | | | | | | | | | | | | |
| | | | | | | | | | | | | | |
| | | | | | | | | | | | | | |
| | | | | | | | | | | | | | |
| Total | | | | | | | | | | | | | |
| **EXPENDITURE** | | | | | | | | | | | | | |
| | | | | | | | | | | | | | |
| | | | | | | | | | | | | | |
| | | | | | | | | | | | | | |
| | | | | | | | | | | | | | |
| | | | | | | | | | | | | | |
| | | | | | | | | | | | | | |
| | | | | | | | | | | | | | |
| | | | | | | | | | | | | | |
| Total | | | | | | | | | | | | | |
| **Surplus/Deficit** | | | | | | | | | | | | | |

## Cash Flow Forecast

| | Apr | May | Jun | Jul | Aug | Sep | Oct | Nov | Dec | Jan | Feb | Mar | Total |
|---|---|---|---|---|---|---|---|---|---|---|---|---|---|
| **RECEIPTS** | | | | | | | | | | | | | |
| | | | | | | | | | | | | | |
| | | | | | | | | | | | | | |
| | | | | | | | | | | | | | |
| | | | | | | | | | | | | | |
| **PAYMENTS** | | | | | | | | | | | | | |
| | | | | | | | | | | | | | |
| | | | | | | | | | | | | | |
| | | | | | | | | | | | | | |
| | | | | | | | | | | | | | |
| **TOTAL** | | | | | | | | | | | | | |
| **Bal. Month** | | | | | | | | | | | | | |
| **Bal. b/f** | | | | | | | | | | | | | |
| **Bal. c/f** | | | | | | | | | | | | | |

# Chapter 8

## KEY FINANCIAL TERMS

### *A*

### Account

A record of financial transactions.

### Accounting Period

The period of time covered by an organisation's accounts. Usually it refers to the financial year, which for many public sector organisations runs from 1$^{st}$ April to 31$^{st}$ March. However, an accounting period may cover any length of time.

### Accounting system

The means by which transactions are recorded thus enabling the production of financial and management accounts.

### Accrual

An accounting entry that reflects the usage of goods or services yet to be invoiced at the end of the accounting period. The accrual estimates the value of such use, and sets up a credit item to reflect that the organisation "owes" the suppliers, even though an official invoice has not yet been received. Accruals are often raised for items such as telephone and utilities, where usage is only billed quarterly.

## Assets

Items the organisation owns, such as property, equipment and cash.

## Audit

An independent examination of an organisation's activities. Audits can be conducted internally or externally by independent audit firms.

Internal audit provides an independent review of activities within the organisation. It is a managerial control mechanism which measures and evaluates the effectiveness of financial and other controls. In some cases it helps to investigate fraud.

External audit provides the independent examination of, and expression of opinion on, the annual financial statements of an organisation. External audits are often required by legislation for companies and public sector organisations.

## Audit Report

A report provided by the external auditors stating their opinion of the financial statements. The report usually includes the term *"the financial statements....present fairly.....the financial position"*.

### B

## Bad Debt

Money owed by customers but written off in the accounts, because it cannot or is unlikely to be collected. Sometimes the term "doubtful debts, or impairment of debtors" may be used.

## Balance Sheet

A statement showing what the organisation owns and owes at any particular time. It lists the nature of the assets and liabilities and shows the **net worth** of the organisation.

## Bank Reconciliation

A statement reconciling the difference between the bank account balance reported on a bank statement, and the same bank account balance appearing in the organisation's books of account.

## Bankruptcy

When an individual cannot, nor has the prospect of being able to meet debts as they become due. This is similar to insolvency for a corporate body. Bankruptcy has to be legally determined in order to become official.

## Books of Account

A set of books which record the financial transactions of an organisation.

## Budget

A financial plan of the estimated income and expenditure over a particular period of time.

## Business Plan

A document setting out an organisation's objectives and how they will be achieved over a specific period of time. This should be used as a management tool and is a result of the business planning process.

## Business Planning Process

This is a process whereby an organisation performs a structured appraisal of its objectives, and analyses its current position with regard to its activities, resources and the environment in which it operates; and develops a set of strategic action plans in order to achieve its objectives, taking into account all the financial implications of those actions.

# *C*

## Capital

Fixed capital is invested in land, buildings, machinery, vehicles, etc.; working capital circulates within the organisation with respect to day to day transactions.

## Capital Expenditure

Expenditure on assets which have a continuing value to the organisation for more than one year, e.g. buildings and equipment.

## Cash Book

A book in which an account (record) is kept of all receipts and payments.

## Cash Flow

Movement of money through the organisation, from buying materials, paying expenses, producing goods and services, selling the service and receiving payment.

## Cash Flow Forecasts

An estimate of the future movement of money through the organisation, to help predict the cash balances throughout the year.

## Closing of Accounts

This usually takes place at the end of a financial year. It requires "closing off" and adjusting all accounts in the financial system, in order to report on income and expenditure for the period. This process is the beginning stage for preparing the financial statements.

## Commitments

Committed expenditure in respect of goods, services and works for which orders have been placed, or contracts agreed, but which have yet to be delivered.

## Contingency

A sum set aside to provide for foreseen but unquantifiable future commitments, or for unforeseen expenditure which may become necessary during the year.

## Cost Centre

The term for an individual area of service to which items of income and expenditure are charged for managerial and financial control purposes. For example, a department, business unit, project, etc.

## Credit

Part of the double entry system (see debit).

## Creditors (accounts payable)

These are the suppliers of goods and services to whom payment is due.

## Current Assets

Usually includes cash, debtors and stock. All realisable within one year.

## Current Liabilities

The amounts owed by the organisation to third parties which are payable within one year.

## *D*

## Debit

Part of the double entry accounting process, opposite to credit. A debit entry is made on the accounting system in relation to an increase in assets; a decrease in liabilities; an increase in expense; or a decrease in income.

## Debtors (accounts receivable)

These are the customers who owe money for goods and services received from the organisation. Customers may include individuals, organisations, or other third parties.

## Depreciation

The rate at which an asset loses its value over time, based on the organisation's accounting policies. For example, vehicles may be depreciated equally over a 4 year period, which means that 25% of the cost is written off to the income and expenditure each year.

## Double-entry

Method of book-keeping in which two entries are made in the books of account for each transaction, reflecting the dual effect every transaction has on the organisation. For example, if a telephone bill is paid it increases the telephone expenditure and decreases the cash asset. These entries are often referred to as debit and credit entries. All accounting systems process transactions in this manner.

## *E*

## Estimate

A method of informing a potential customer of the approximate price of your goods and services. It is a carefully worked out approximation, not a fixed price, and allows for changes if necessary. *(i.e. giving an estimate for the cost of goods or services)*

Also, refers to the process used when developing budget and forecasts when actual figures are unknown.

## *F*

## Financial Regulations

A written set of rules and guidance agreed by an organisation to provide a framework in which to conduct its financial affairs. These are required for good governance.

## Financial Statements

These consist of at least the income and expenditure account, and balance sheet, along with notes to the accounts. They cover a specific period of time, usually one year. They are the product of an organisation's financial systems and are usually subject to external audit.

## Fixed Assets

These are the assets with continuing value, usually more than one year, such as land, premises, plant, equipment and machinery.

## Fixed Costs

These are costs which do not vary with output or productivity in the short term, such as rent.

## Forecast

An expression of an organisation's long term plan in financial terms. The forecast predicts future income and expenditure. The two main forecasts used in planning are the income and expenditure forecast and cash flow forecast.

## G

## General Ledger

The principal book of account consolidating all the other books of account, such as the cash book, purchase ledger, sales ledger, and so on.

## Going Concern

The status whereby the organisation is in a financial position to continue its operations into the foreseeable future.

## Goodwill

This is an intangible asset, and represents a value that an organisation is prepared to place on a business or entity which may be over and above its cost.

## Gross

A total without any deductions.

## Gross Profit

Sales or turnover for a period, less the direct cost of sales, excluding overheads.

## *H*

## Historic Cost

Fixed assets are normally shown at historic cost in the balance sheet; the cost at which they were originally purchased. Some assets are re-valued on a regular basis, e.g. land and property.

## *I*

## Income

Amounts generated by an organisation which have been received or are receivable. Public sector income includes grants, rents, sales, fees and charges.

## Inflation

This is the effect brought about by rising prices, which reduces the value of money.

## Insolvent

When an organisation's assets are worth less than its liabilities, and it is unable to meet its liabilities when they fall due.

## Insurance

Protection against risk. Organisations can purchase specialist insurance policies to ensure against almost all kinds of risk (at a price). Some large organisations "self-insure" as they can afford to cover the consequences of some risk factors.

## Intangible Assets

These are assets which have no physical existence, e.g. an asset which is neither fixed nor current, yet possesses a value, such as goodwill, copyright or intellectual property.

## Invoice

A document showing the character, quantity, price, terms, nature of delivery and other particulars of goods sold or services rendered.

## *J*

## Journal Entry

An adjustment to the main books of account. Journals entries are used for changes such as correcting errors or allocating expenditure between different cost centres. They are also made at the end of a financial year to assist with the closing of accounts.

## L

### Liability

An amount owed to an individual or organisation which will be paid at some time in the future. Liabilities include loans, creditors, leases, overdrafts, and so on.

### Liquid Assets

These include cash and easily realisable assets, such as debtors or short-term investments.

### Liquidity

A measure of an organisation's ability to pay its current liabilities as they fall due.

## M

### Management Accounts

These are internal tailor-made financial statements and reports prepared as required. They assist management to control the organisation's financial resources on a day to day basis, and help to inform their decision making.

## N

### Net Book Value

Represents the value of fixed assets at a point in time. It is calculated as cost less accumulated depreciation.

### Net Profit

The profit gained after deducting overheads from gross profit.

## Net Worth

Also known as net assets. This figure is found by adding fixed assets plus net current assets or working capital (current assets - current liabilities) less long term liabilities.

## Nominal Ledger

Otherwise known as the general ledger.

## O

## Overheads

Sometimes referred to as administrative or support costs, such as legal, personnel, finance, etc. Unlike operational or direct costs, these cannot always be directly allocated to a particular area of service.

## P

## Petty Cash

Money used for small cash transactions. Most organisations have a financial limit for petty cash.

## Profit and Loss Account

This statement is usually prepared by businesses and organisations operating in the private sector. It shows the income and expenditure from a trading activity for a specific period resulting in either profit or loss. This is similar to the income and expenditure account prepared by many public and not for profit organisations, where the balance is referred to as a surplus or deficit.

## Provisions

Amounts set aside for potential and specific liabilities known to the organisation at the time of the preparation of the accounts. For example, provision for depreciation and bad debts. Provisions have the impact of reducing surpluses and are created using a journal entry.

## *R*

## Recharge

An internal transaction whereby one cost centre recharges another cost centre for services provided.

## Revenue Expenditure

The day to day expenses an organisation incurs in providing its services (as opposed to capital expenditure).

## *S*

## Solvent

A situation where an organisation is able to meet all of its short and long term liabilities, i.e. where its assets exceed its liabilities

## Standing Orders

Formal rules an organisation draws up to regulate its proceedings and the conduct of its activities. Standing orders will cover all key areas including finance.

## Suspense Account

An account which is used for amounts that cannot immediately be correctly allocated to a specific account or cost centre. This is usually because of inadequate information.

## *T*

## Tangible Assets

These are assets with a physical existence such as land, premises, plant, equipment etc.

## *U*

## Unit Cost

The cost of one unit of service, such as cost per hour, cost per pupil, cost per dwelling, etc.

## *V*

## Variable Costs

Costs which vary with productivity, i.e. in accordance with the volume or level of service provided.

## Variance

The differences between actual and budgeted figures.

## Viability

The ability of an organisation to sustain its existence into the long term, by ensuring it can continue to generate sufficient income to cover its costs.

## Virement

The transfer of funds from one budget head to another, in accordance with an organisation's financial regulations and standing orders. This adjustment is often made to correct a budget area that is or may become overspent. It is used as part of the financial management control process.

## *W*

## Working Capital

The sums available to meet the day to day expense of maintaining an operation. Working capital is usually calculated as current assets less current liabilities.

## *Z*

## Zero Growth

No additional growth in budgets over that of the previous year.

# SOLUTIONS TO EXERCISES

# Solutions to Exercises

# Solution to Exercise 1
## Accounting Entries

a) A fire officer purchases new uniforms for £10,000 but has yet to pay the supplier.

| Increase in expenditure account on uniforms | £10,000 |
|---|---|
| Increase in creditors (people we owe money to) | £10,000 |

b) A doctor charges £50 for writing a letter on behalf of a client for which the client had to pay in advance.

| Increase in fees | £50 |
|---|---|
| Increase in cash | £50 |

c) A school contracts out its cleaning services to a private contractor and has to pay £24,000 a year in monthly instalments. Show the entries for this month.

| Increase in expenditure on cleaning contract | £2,000 |
|---|---|
| Decrease in cash | £2,000 |

d) The planning department advised three clients during the week all of whom were charged £200 each for advice. Two paid immediately, however, the third has yet to pay.

| Increase in fees | £600 |
|---|---|
| Increase in cash | £400 |
| Increase in debtors (people who owe us money) | £200 |

e) Three managers of a day care centre service, decide to set up their own company in order to bid independently for contracts. To make the initial start, they all invest £10,000 each in the new company.

| Increase in cash | £30,000 |
|---|---|
| Increase in owners' equity (could use the term capital or investment) | £30,000 |

# Solution to Exercise 3
## Which Financial Statement?

|  | Income and Expenditure | Balance Sheet |
|---|---|---|
| Cash in bank |  | X |
| Fees | X |  |
| Motor vehicles |  | X |
| Creditors |  | X |
| Stationery | X |  |
| Rent | X |  |
| Grants | X |  |
| Overdraft |  | X |
| Computer maintenance | X |  |
| Depreciation | X |  |
| Debtors |  | X |
| Office furniture |  | X |
| Insurance | X |  |
| Loan |  | X |
| Bank interest | X |  |
| Salaries | X |  |
| Reserves |  | X |

# Solution to Exercise 4
## Preparing a Trading Account

|  | £ | £ |
|---|---|---|
| Income: |  |  |
| Fees |  | 180,000 |
| Expenditure: |  |  |
| Direct costs | 45,000 |  |
| Consultant fees | 20,000 |  |
| Salaries | 38,000 |  |
| Office Overheads | 6,000 |  |
| Other charges | 5,000 |  |
| Loan interest (5% of £100,000) | 5,000 |  |
| Depreciation | 15,000 |  |
| Total |  | 134,000 |
| Surplus or Deficit for the year |  | 46,000 |

# Solution to Exercise 5
## Preparing an Income and Expenditure Account

**Limit H.A.**
***Income and Expenditure Account***
***for the year ended 20XX***

---

**Limit H.A.**
**Income and Expenditure Account**
**for the year ended 19XX**

**INCOME**

| | | |
|---|---|---|
| Trading and Operations | 1,950,000 | |
| Other income (interest) | 15,000 | |
| | | 1,965,000 |

**EXPENDITURE**

| | | |
|---|---|---|
| Direct Expenditure | 1,885,000 | |
| Central Costs | 45,000 | |
| Interest Payments | 65,000 | |
| Depreciation | 10,000 | |
| | | 2,005,000 |
| Deficit for the Year | | **(40,000)** |

---

# Solution to Exercise 8
## Preparing the Balance Sheet

| | Cost £ | Depreciation £ | NBV £ | |
|---|---|---|---|---|
| **Fixed Assets** | | | | |
| Equipment | 100,000 | 15,000 | 85,000 | A |
| **Current Assets** | | | | |
| Debtors | 72,000 | | | |
| Cash | 0 | | | |
| (sub total x) | | 72,000 | | |
| **Current Liabilities** | | | | |
| Creditors | 0 | | | |
| Overdraft | 11,000 | | | |
| (sub total y) | | 11,000 | | |
| **Net Current Assets** (x-y) | | | 61,000 | B |
| Net Assets | | | 146,000 | A+B |
| **Represented by** | | | | |
| Surplus for the year from the trading account | | 46,000 | | |
| Loan | | 100,000 | | |
| (A+B) should equal C | | | 146,000 | C |

## *Calculation Notes:*

1.  Calculate the cash balance for the year as follows:

    | | |
    |---|---|
    | Cash Received (£180,000-40% outstanding £72,000) | £108,000 |
    | Cash paid (all the expenditure less the depreciation) | £119,000 |
    | Overdraft | -£11,000 |

2.  Calculate the debtors 40% of £180,000      £72,000

3.  Calculate the depreciation 15% of £100,000      £15,000
    and subtract from the cost of the
    equipment to give a net book value (NBV)      £85,000

4.  Surplus was calculated from exercise 4      £46,000

# Solution to Exercise 9
## Calculating Key Financial Ratios

|  | Year 1 | Year 2 |
|---|---|---|
| a) R.O.C.E. | $\dfrac{16,000}{100,000}$ <br> = 16% | $\dfrac{17,000}{100,000}$ <br> = 17% |
| Surplus Percentage | $\dfrac{16,000}{600,000}$ <br> = 2.67% | $\dfrac{17,000}{700,000}$ <br> = 2.43% |

Income Growth

$$\frac{700,000 - 600,000}{600,000}$$
$$= 16.67\%$$

b)  Additional information needed should include:

- Budget Information - planned income and expenditure
- Performance Targets - planned rates of return
- Business Plan - planned service output
- Balance Sheet - liquidity levels, especially level of debtors

# Solution to Exercise 10
## Interpretation of Financial Ratios

An argument could be made for both health centres to remain open, particularly as they are both making a surplus. However, if one does have to close then based on the information given at face value it should be health centre 1, for the following reasons:

*   It has a higher capital base (£50,000[1] compared with £24,000[2]) and hence releases more capital on closure.

    | (1) | $\dfrac{5,000}{10\%}$ | (2) | $\dfrac{600}{2.5\%}$ |
    |---|---|---|---|

*   There is a low liquidity level, and even more worrying is the high level of debtors, and slow debt collection rates compared to the other health centre (110, compared with 73 days)

*   Even though both health centres have a negative variance on their budgeted surplus, health centre 1 is significantly higher, especially given that the increase in productivity is only half a percent compared with the 6 percent of health centre 2.

What is clear is that a number of other factors would affect the decision such as:

*   **Location of the centres**
    Impact on cost, impact on number of users, etc.

*   **Number of users**
    Impact on cost

*   **Physical condition**
    Potential need for refurbishment could lead to greater cost

*   **Maximum capacity**
    Impact on the potential for expansion to cope with effect of closure of the other health centre

# Solution to Exercise 11
## Understanding Your Cash Flow

| Question | Score | Question | Score | Question | Score |
|---|---|---|---|---|---|
| 1 a | 2 | 2 a | 4 | 3 a | 4 |
| b | 1 | b | 2 | b | 1 |
| c | 4 | | | | |
| d | 3 | | | | |
| 4 a | 4 | 5 a | 1 | 6 a | 1 |
| b | 2 | b | 2 | b | 3 |
| c | 3 | c | 4 | c | 4 |
| 7 a | 4 | 8 a | 3 | 9 a | 1 |
| B | 2 | b | 1 | b | 3 |
| 10 a | 4 | | | | |
| b | 2 | | | | |
| c | 1 | | | | |

## Over 25

Cash seems to be very tight within the organisation, and even slight delays in the timing of cash receipts could cause a cash crisis. The organisation should always make sure that a cash flow forecast is produced and updated regularly such that the extent of any overdraft requirements are known well in advance. If possible, the organisation should arrange overdraft facilities that are in excess of their needs to prevent the chances of cash flow difficulties. The organisation should also examine its sources of funds and try to maximise the speed of cash collection using effective credit control procedures.

## 16 to 25

Cash flow seems to be stable and does not present a problem at the moment. However, the organisation is not sufficiently robust to ignore the timing of cash receipts and payments. There is a need for close monitoring of balances to ensure that the cash position always remains in control.

## 15 or less

The organisation does not have any problems with cash levels and appears to be in a very strong position with regard to cash flows. The organisation has to concentrate its efforts on treasury management and ensuring that it maximises the income earned by any cash surpluses.

# Solution to Exercise 12
## Preparing an Income and Expenditure Forecast

| | Apr | May | Jun | Jul | Aug | Sep | Oct | Nov | Dec | Jan | Feb | Mar | Total |
|---|---|---|---|---|---|---|---|---|---|---|---|---|---|
| **Income (£'000)** | | | | | | | | | | | | | |
| Grant | 12.0 | | | 12.0 | | | 12.0 | | | 12.0 | | | 48.0 |
| Fees | 14.0 | 14.0 | 14.0 | 14.0 | 14.0 | 14.0 | 14.0 | 14.0 | 14.0 | 14.0 | 14.0 | 14.0 | 168.0 |
| Fund-raising | 0.2 | 0.2 | 0.2 | 0.2 | 0.2 | 0.2 | 0.2 | 0.2 | 0.2 | 0.2 | 0.2 | 0.2 | 2.4 |
| Donation | 0.1 | 0.1 | 0.1 | 0.1 | 0.1 | 0.1 | 0.1 | 0.1 | 0.1 | 0.1 | 0.1 | 0.1 | 1.2 |
| Total | 26.3 | 14.3 | 14.3 | 26.3 | 14.3 | 14.3 | 26.3 | 14.3 | 14.3 | 26.3 | 14.3 | 14.3 | 219.6 |
| **Expend. (£,000)** | | | | | | | | | | | | | |
| Salaries | 13.0 | 13.0 | 13.0 | 13.0 | 13.0 | 13.0 | 13.0 | 13.0 | 13.0 | 13.0 | 13.0 | 13.0 | 156.0 |
| Catering | 1.2 | 1.2 | 1.2 | 1.2 | 1.2 | 1.2 | 1.2 | 1.2 | 1.2 | 1.2 | 1.2 | 1.2 | 14.4 |
| Uniforms | | | | | | 2.0 | | | | | | 2.0 | 4.0 |
| Toys | 0.4 | 0.4 | 0.4 | 0.4 | 0.4 | 0.4 | 0.4 | 0.4 | 0.4 | 0.4 | 0.4 | 0.4 | 4.8 |
| Supplies & Services | 1.0 | 1.0 | 1.0 | 1.0 | 1.0 | 1.0 | 1.0 | 1.0 | 1.0 | 1.0 | 1.0 | 1.0 | 12.0 |
| Rent | 5.0 | | | 5.0 | | | 5.0 | | | 5.0 | | | 20.0 |
| Sundry | 0.5 | 0.5 | 0.5 | 0.5 | 0.5 | 0.5 | 0.5 | 0.5 | 0.5 | 0.5 | 0.5 | 0.5 | 6.0 |
| Total | 21.1 | 16.1 | 16.1 | 21.1 | 16.1 | 18.1 | 21.1 | 16.1 | 16.1 | 21.1 | 16.1 | 18.1 | 217.2 |
| Surplus/-Deficit | 5.2 | -1.8 | -1.8 | 5.2 | -1.8 | -3.8 | 5.2 | -1.8 | -1.8 | 5.2 | -1.8 | -3.8 | 2.4 |

# Solution to Exercise 13
## Preparing a Cash Flow Forecast

| | Apr | May | Jun | Jul | Aug | Sep | Oct | Nov | Dec | Jan | Feb | Mar | Total |
|---|---|---|---|---|---|---|---|---|---|---|---|---|---|
| **Income (£'000)** | | | | | | | | | | | | | |
| Grant | 12.0 | | | 12.0 | | | 12.0 | | | 12.0 | | | 48.0 |
| Fees | 11.2 | 14.0 | 14.0 | 14.0 | 14.0 | 14.0 | 14.0 | 14.0 | 14.0 | 14.0 | 14.0 | 14.0 | 165.2 |
| Fund-raising | 0.2 | 0.2 | 0.2 | 0.2 | 0.2 | 0.2 | 0.2 | 0.2 | 0.2 | 0.2 | 0.2 | 0.2 | 2.4 |
| Donation | | | | | | | | | 0.6 | | | 0.6 | 1.2 |
| Total | 23.4 | 14.2 | 14.2 | 26.2 | 14.2 | 14.2 | 26.2 | 14.2 | 14.8 | 26.2 | 14.2 | 14.8 | 216.8 |
| **Expend. (£,000)** | | | | | | | | | | | | | |
| Salaries | 13.0 | 13.0 | 13.0 | 13.0 | 13.0 | 13.0 | 13.0 | 13.0 | 13.0 | 13.0 | 13.0 | 13.0 | 156.0 |
| Catering | 1.2 | 1.2 | 1.2 | 1.2 | 1.2 | 1.2 | 1.2 | 1.2 | 1.2 | 1.2 | 1.2 | 1.2 | 14.4 |
| Uniforms | | | | | | | 2.0 | | | | | | 2.0 |
| Toys | | 0.4 | 0.4 | 0.4 | 0.4 | 0.4 | 0.4 | 0.4 | 0.4 | 0.4 | 0.4 | 0.4 | 4.4 |
| Supplies & Services | | 1.0 | 1.0 | 1.0 | 1.0 | 1.0 | 1.0 | 1.0 | 1.0 | 1.0 | 1.0 | 1.0 | 11.0 |
| Rent | 5.0 | | | 5.0 | | | 5.0 | | | 5.0 | | | 20.0 |
| Sundry | 0.5 | 0.5 | 0.5 | 0.5 | 0.5 | 0.5 | 0.5 | 0.5 | 0.5 | 0.5 | 0.5 | 0.5 | 6.0 |
| Total | 19.7 | 16.1 | 16.1 | 21.1 | 16.1 | 16.1 | 23.1 | 16.1 | 16.1 | 21.1 | 16.1 | 16.1 | 213.8 |
| Balance mth | 3.7 | -1.9 | -1.9 | 5.1 | -1.9 | -1.9 | 3.1 | -1.9 | -1.3 | 5.1 | -1.9 | -1.3 | 3.0 |
| Cash b/f | 0 | 3.7 | 1.8 | -0.1 | 5.0 | 3.1 | 1.2 | 4.3 | 2.4 | 1.1 | 6.2 | 4.3 | 0 |
| Cash c/f | 3.7 | 1.8 | -0.1 | 5.0 | 3.1 | 1.2 | 4.3 | 2.4 | 1.1 | 6.2 | 4.3 | 3.0 | 3.0 |

# Solution to Exercise 14
## Re-Forecasting

| | Apr | May | Jun | Jul | Aug | Sep | Oct | Nov | Dec | Jan | Feb | Mar | Total |
|---|---|---|---|---|---|---|---|---|---|---|---|---|---|
| **Income** | | | | | | | | | | | | | |
| **(£'000)** | | | | | | | | | | | | | |
| Grant | | 12.0 | | | 12.0 | | | 12.0 | | | 12.0 | | 48.0 |
| Fees | 11.2 | 14.0 | 14.0 | 14.0 | 14.0 | 14.0 | 14.0 | 14.0 | 14.0 | 14.0 | 14.0 | 14.0 | 165.2 |
| Fund-raising | | | | | 0.2 | 0.2 | 0.2 | 0.2 | 0.2 | 0.2 | 0.2 | 0.2 | 1.6 |
| Donation | | | | | | | | | 0.6 | | | 0.6 | 1.2 |
| Total | 11.2 | 26.0 | 14.0 | 14.0 | 26.2 | 14.2 | 14.2 | 26.2 | 14.8 | 14.2 | 26.2 | 14.8 | 216.0 |
| **Expend.** | | | | | | | | | | | | | |
| **(£,000)** | | | | | | | | | | | | | |
| Salaries | 13.0 | 13.0 | 13.0 | 13.0 | 13.0 | 13.0 | 13.0 | 13.0 | 13.0 | 13.0 | 13.0 | 13.0 | 156.0 |
| Catering | 1.0 | 1.0 | 1.0 | 1.0 | 1.0 | 1.0 | 1.0 | 1.0 | 1.0 | 1.0 | 1.0 | 1.0 | 12.0 |
| Uniforms | | | | | | 2.0 | | | | | | | 2.0 |
| Toys | | 0.4 | 0.4 | 0.4 | 0.4 | 0.4 | 0.4 | 0.4 | 0.4 | 0.4 | 0.4 | 0.4 | 4.4 |
| Supplies & | | 1.2 | 1.2 | 1.2 | 1.2 | 1.2 | 1.2 | 1.2 | 1.2 | 1.2 | 1.2 | 1.2 | 13.2 |
| Services | | | | | | | | | | | | | |
| Rent | 5.0 | | | 5.0 | | | 5.0 | | | 5.0 | | | 20.0 |
| Sundry | 0.5 | 0.5 | 0.5 | 0.5 | 0.5 | 0.5 | 0.5 | 0.5 | 0.5 | 0.5 | 0.5 | 0.5 | 6.0 |
| Total | 19.7 | 16.1 | 16.1 | 21.1 | 16.1 | 16.1 | 23.1 | 16.1 | 16.1 | 21.1 | 16.1 | 16.1 | 213.6 |
| | | | | | | | | | | | | | |
| Balance mth | -8.3 | 9.9 | -2.1 | -7.1 | 10.1 | -1.9 | -8.9 | 10.1 | -1.3 | -6.9 | 10.1 | -1.3 | 2.4 |
| Cash b/f | 0 | -8.3 | 1.6 | -0.5 | -7.6 | 2.5 | 0.6 | -8.3 | 1.8 | 0.5 | -6.4 | 3.7 | 0 |
| Cash c/f | -8.3 | 1.6 | -0.5 | -7.6 | 2.5 | 0.6 | -8.3 | 1.8 | 0.5 | -6.4 | 3.7 | 2.4 | 2.4 |

Overdraft facilities would be in excess of **£8,300**

# INDEX

# A

# B

# C

# D

# E

# F

# G

# I

# J

# L

# M

# N

Net Book Value · 107
Net Worth · 40, 108

# O

Outsourcing · 1, 28, 51
Overdraft · 63
Overheads · 108, 110

# P

Performance Measure · 23, 49
Prepayments · 22, 29
Profit · 47, 107
Profit and Loss Account · 108
Provisions · 62, 109

# Q

Quick Ratio · 55

# R

Rate of return · 50, 51, 53, 58, 68, 80
Recharges · 109
Reserves · 40
Return on Capital Employed (ROCE) · 50, 52
Return on Investment (ROI) · 50
Revenue account · 9
Revenue Expenditure · 20

# S

Setting Objectives · 75
Share Capital · 42
Solvent · 109

## T

## U

## V

## W

For further information see www.hbpublications.com
and www.fci-system.com